CW01480930

AN ENDURING FRIENDSHIP

400 YEARS OF
ANGLO-GULF RELATIONS

AN ENDURING FRIENDSHIP

Copyright © Windsor Energy Group 2006

Stacey International Publishers
128 Kensington Church Street
London W8 4BH
Telephone: 020 7221 7166 Fax: 020 7792 9288
E-mail: marketing@stacey-international.co.uk
www.stacey-international.co.uk

ISBN: 1-905299-18-4

CIP Data: A catalogue record for this book is available from the British Library

Editor: Paul Tempest

Printing & Binding: Cambridge University Press

AN ENDURING FRIENDSHIP

400 YEARS OF
ANGLO-GULF RELATIONS

EDITED BY PAUL TEMPEST

STACEY INTERNATIONAL

CONTENTS

PREFACE

This volume is dedicated as a memorial to the life and achievement of the Hon. Sir David Alwyn Gore-Booth KCMG, KCVO. Its objective is to provide an authoritative record of the political, commercial and cultural relations established between Britain and the countries of the Arab Gulf over a period of 400 years, to assess the state of the relationship today and to identify some of the opportunities ahead.

First, a word about David Gore-Booth. In his career, tragically cut short by cancer in October 2004, David played, with consummate diplomacy and a warm heart, his own significant part in strengthening this strong relationship between Britain and the Gulf.

On retirement from the Foreign Service in 1999, David became Special Adviser to the Chairman of the Hong Kong and Shanghai Banking Corporation (HSBC) specialising in relations with the 22 member Governments of the Arab League and travelling frequently to the kingdoms of Saudi Arabia and Bahrain, to the emirates of Kuwait, Qatar and the UAE and to the sultanate of Oman. He also helped found the Windsor Energy Group (WEG) in 1999 and served as its Chairman until his death in October 2004. In this volume we reproduce an amalgam of his lecture notes compiled and delivered between 2000 and 2004 under the title he selected, 'The Middle East – Myths and Realities'.

Here we have asked a selected number of David Gore-Booth's former ambassadorial colleagues to compile a concise history of the relationship between the UK and the country in the Gulf to which they were accredited. The aim is to try to capture the essentials of that relationship. Each produced a lecture before an invited WEG audience and a text for publication.

To start the process, we invited Sir James Craig to deliver an opening Memorial Lecture on the British and the Arabs with a strong emphasis placed by the British Government on their diplomats acquiring a command of spoken and written Arabic and a deep understanding of Arab culture and Islamic civilisation. Then followed lectures on Kuwait, Bahrain, the UAE, Oman and Qatar.

The second stage of the project is to add three more extensive studies on the three larger remaining states of the Gulf, namely Saudi Arabia, Iraq and Iran. Already, we are discussing with our members how the authorship, each by one or more former British Ambassadors, should be structured. Also there will be specialist contributions on Trade, Banking, Investment, Oil and Gas Development, Industrial Diversification and Tourism with ample maps, photographs and the latest statistics.

The third stage (only at present in embryo), is to extend the coverage of the Arab Gulf states to all 22 member countries of the Arab league and to provide thereby a comprehensive and authoritative guide and gazetteer to the Middle East.

In the preparation of this volume and in the regular series of discussions of the issues raised, the Windsor Energy Group would like to express their sincere thanks to the four London Ambassadors who have been unfailing in their support, attendance and encouragement of the Windsor Energy Group and of this project: HE Khaled al-Duwaisan GCVO, *Dean of the London Diplomatic Corps, and Ambassador of Kuwait in London since 1993,* HE Nasser bin Hamad al-Khalifa, *Ambassador of Qatar in London 2000-2005 and now Qatar Ambassador to the USA,* HE HRH Prince Turki al-Faisal, *Ambassador of the Kingdom of Saudi Arabia in London 2003-2005 and now Ambassador to the USA,* HE Shaikh Khalid bin Ahmed al Khalifa, *Ambassador of Bahrain in London 2001-2005 and now the Foreign Minister of Bahrain.*

THE MIDDLE EAST: MYTHS AND REALITIES

David Gore-Booth

To most casual observers the Middle East conjures up visions not of a Thousand and One Nights but of Mullahs, Murderers and Mayhem — an image reinforced by the terrible events of 11 September 2001 in New York and Washington. As such it seems to have spawned more myths than any other region in the world. Which is why I thought it worth addressing a few of them. If we can separate the myths from the realities we may be on course to identifying the way forward.

Myths

ISLAM

Priests there are aplenty, most obviously in Iran, Saudi Arabia and Israel whilst the mosque is of course ubiquitous throughout the Arab world. But the notion that there is an Islamic Comintern hard at subterranean work in the region – or that it is part of an inevitable clash between Islam and the West – is pure fantasy: as fantastic in fact as the notion that the Prophet Mohammed was a bloodthirsty zealot rather than a peace monger who united the feuding tribes of Arabia. To quote Edward Said:

> There isn't a single Islam: there are Islams, just as there are Americans. This diversity is true of all traditions, religions or Nations even though some of their adherents have futilely tried to draw boundaries around themselves and pin their creeds down neatly.

7

Of course, Islam, like all religions, has its fundamentalist wing. But fundamentalism feeds on failure and it is failure that has fed Islamic fundamentalism – whether of the West in bringing peace to the region or of the region itself in adjusting to modernisation. I subscribe to the view that it is not true, as Westerners sometimes imagine, that Islam makes it impossible for Muslims to create a modern secular society.

JERUSALEM

There are religious flashpoints of course – the most obvious being Jerusalem. There the myth is that somehow it all belongs to Israel, whereas the reality is that Muslims and Christians in a religious sense and Palestinians in a political sense have an equal claim. The city will have to be shared if there is to be peace in the Middle East. I cannot put it better than the distinguished William Pfaff:

> The only possibilities are to share Sovereignty, or renounce it in favour of an international authority. Unless one of those solutions can be agreed upon, nothing has been resolved. That is what Palestinians and Israelis have discovered, but have yet to come to terms with.

PEACE SETTLEMENT

Do both sides want peace? The myth is that Israel does and that the Arabs reject it. That may have been true in 1967, but the Arabs have learned through three wars and umpteen skirmishes that they cannot erase Israel from the map. Yet the traffic in Israel has been in the other direction. It is now Israel that is in danger. Douglas Hurd described the problem thus:

> Israel was allowed to follow in the twentieth century a policy comparable with that of expansionist powers in the nineteenth. In so doing Israel has prevented herself from achieving the peace settlement that would in fact suit her best: division between Israel and a Palestinian state roughly on the lines of the 1967 border.

The myth is that the Palestinians need peace more than Israel does. The reality is that the Palestinians have suffered so much and waited so long that they can afford to suffer more and wait longer for a just settlement. Israel cannot afford to let this sore run on without grave damage to its polity, society and reputation.

DEMOCRACY

The notion that Israel is the only proper democracy in the Middle East is under increasing scrutiny and, in the eyes of this observer, some threat. Elections are held in many Arab countries. I am not talking about the 99 per cent variety in such as Syria and formerly Iraq, but the much more genuine variety in Lebanon, Kuwait, Egypt, Jordan, Algeria, Morocco and Tunisia. The very governability of Israel may be at issue. There is clearly a problem. As Uri Dromi, who was actually in government, put it:

> With the current, ill-advised electoral system, Israelis have lost the ability to compromise. We, therefore, have to come back to our senses and replace this disastrous system with something that works.

Clearly some serious reassessment is required of what was thought to be a reality but may be becoming a myth.

STRATEGIC ASSET

Another issue in need of serious reassessment is the idea that in some way Israel is a strategic asset to the United States in the Middle East. I have tried hard over many years to intellectualise this. But I have to admit to failure. Israel may have been a strategic asset to Britain and France in the Suez affair in 1956 – yet it was the United States that undermined the Franco-British operation and obliged Israel to withdraw. So not much of an asset then. The June 1967 war, which ended with Israel in control of large swathes of Egypt, Jordan and Syria, did huge damage to the West's – and above all America's – position in the Middle East: the 1973 war would have done likewise had Washington not expended much political capital in contriving the Camp David Agreement: the 1978 and 1982 Israeli invasions of the Lebanon caused successive US Secretaries of State endless frustration. And to prove the point beyond gainsay the US had to beg the Israelis not to intervene in the Gulf crisis of 1990/91 in order to preserve the 30-member coalition it had assembled against Iraq.

The same factor has been at work following the ghastly events of 11 September 2001: the Americans realise they cannot assemble a broad coalition against terrorism if it includes Israel. The reality is that Israel needs to treat itself as – and be treated as – just another Middle Eastern State and not either a 51st state of the United States or a putative member state of the European Union.

OIL

The myth, carefully propagated by Western Governments in difficulty in the seventies, is that OPEC is a coherent group of rapacious third-worlders determined to squeeze Western economies until their pips squeak. The reality is that OPEC is a highly disparate bunch of countries from several continents who have great difficulty coordinating. They agree on two things: that they should receive a fair and stable price for their commodity (which is often their only resource), and secondly that it is hypocritical of Western governments to cry foul when, as in the case of the UK, 75 per cent of the price of a gallon on the forecourt goes to the Exchequer and not to the producer.

INSTABILITY

The received wisdom seems to be that the Middle East is inherently unstable. Of course there have been lurches here and there. Revolutions plagued the region in the post-war period as it emerged from the colonial embrace. But the last one of these was in 1979.

King Hussein of Jordan survived almost fifty years at the epicentre of the Arab-Israel conflict. President Assad of Syria survived 30 years at a similar focal point and has been succeeded by another President Assad. The ghastly Saddam Hussein was at the top of the pole in Iraq for almost 35 years, despite defeats in the two wars of expansion against Iran and Kuwait. President Mubarak is, as I write, in his third seven-year term.

King Hassan ruled Morocco for over 30 years and was succeeded by his son.

Even the notably erratic Colonel Qadhafi has been in charge of Libya for well over 30 years (having defied the prediction of the

British Embassy, including Second Secretary Gore-Booth, that he could not last more than six months).

The problem in the Arab world in general is not too much change – it is too little.

SANCTIONS

This blurring of US and Israeli interests in the region has too often led Washington to impose sanctions on various states in the region. For a country that aspires to be everybody's friend – to export its model of society across the globe – it is odd to say the least that Uncle Sam has sanctions of one kind or another in place against such as Iran, Syria, Sudan and Libya. Sanctions are a very unsubtle weapon to use in what is a very subtle part of the world. Too often, they provide, as in Iraq, wholly unsavoury characters with a means to strengthen their grip on wretched citizens – which is exactly the opposite of the intention: myth one way, reality the other.

EU v US

I suppose, as a European, that the United States excluded itself for so long from a large slice of Middle Eastern territory for good reason. But I am not sure whether this was wise or not. Because I do believe that the Middle East deserves a major infusion of Western culture, I do not mean Coca-Cola colonisation – and in any case Coke and Pepsi are already available throughout the area. I do mean that the Middle East needs political, economic, social and, dare I say it, religious freedom.

I do believe that there are stirrings in this direction. They would be greatly nourished by a settlement between Israel and its neighbours and have been revived by the departure of Saddam Hussein. If the EU keeps tugging at Uncle Sam's sleeve it is because the Middle East is Europe's underbelly. There are millions of people out there who deserve a better life. We in the West owe it to them – and to ourselves, whether European or American – to maximise their chances of finding it.

GLOBALISATION AND THE MIDDLE EAST

Globalisation is seen by some as in some way the enemy of progress, a barrier to growth with social justice. The reality is that globalisation is the best thing that has happened to the developing world – in the Middle East or anywhere else. The Arab world is coming to the conclusion that neither state socialism – of the Nasserist variety – nor state capitalism – of the old Gulf variety provides an adequate foundation for the future. Privatisation is at work from both ends of the ideological spectrum. As this process gathers momentum it will change Arab economies – and Arab societies – with it, for the better.

The final myth is more than this. It is the myth that the Middle East does not matter, so we can forget about it. The reality is quite different as tragedies in or connected to the region repeatedly demonstrate. Of course the Middle East matters for positive as well as negative reasons.

Realities

Only by distinguishing between myths and realities – and by exposing both – is it possible to discern a path towards peace. This will require greater candour in the West and in the region, whether in Israel or in the Arab world. The West needs to accept, to quote Douglas Hurd again that:

> The key to the dilemma remains the Israeli settlements in the Occupied Territories. Looking back, we have all been remiss in failing to intervene effectively against the spread of these settlements. We have often criticised them as unwise and illegal: there are plenty of harsh words on the record. But the fact of American domestic politics, the guilty feelings of many Europeans towards Israel – the dependence of friendly Arabs on the US have inhibited all of us from making our criticisms effective. As a result the hated settlements have leapt from hillside to hillside.

In Israel there is a need to accept that the Palestinians are there to stay – that Golda Meir's attempt to pretend that they do not exist is invalid – and that co-existence is the only viable solution.

Coexistence between Israelis and Palestinians outside Israel and coexistence between Israelis and Palestinians inside Israel – as Fareed Zakaria puts it:

> The real danger to Israel's democracy is its relationship with its Arab citizens. Israel's biggest problem is not the Arabs in the Occupied Territories. It is the 1.2 million Arabs within Israel... if Israel cannot produce normality in its own Arab population, whatever it does with the Palestinians will be irrelevant. It will find itself having to choose between being Jewish and being a democracy. This is the real time bomb ticking within the borders of Israel.

In Arabia there needs to be a new openness.

Of course Arab societies and traditions do not lend themselves readily to the 'let it all hang out' version of public life that the information revolution – in particular television and the tabloids – have imposed upon us.

Something has changed in the world. The sooner this is understood in Israel, the better. Israel always considered itself different from other countries, was acknowledged as different and was different.

Israel is not different any more and should not be treated as such. The Israeli occupation of East Jerusalem, the West Bank and (until 2005) Gaza is just that – an occupation. It has been allowed to last well over 30 years – as though the Allies had still been occupying West Germany into the eighties. The Palestinians do not want, and are not asking for 'concessions' from Israel. They want 'compliance' with signed agreements, international law and UN resolutions. As Margaret Thatcher once put it, 'the Israelis cannot deny to the Palestinians what they have claimed for themselves.'

THE SIX DAVID GORE-BOOTH MEMORIAL PAPERS

THE BRITISH AND THE ARABS

James Craig

For a long time there was a belief – and it may still survive in some quarters – that there is a special relationship between the British and the Arabs. I don't think that that relationship has ever been defined or indeed that it is definable, even by those who propound it. But it seems to suggest, rather vaguely, that the British and the Arabs understand and respect each other and get on well together.

Here, for example, is a quotation from H V Morton, a popular travel writer of the 1930s, writing in Palestine: 'I can perceive the bond of sympathy and mutual respect that could exist between Bedouin and Englishmen. The desert, I think, is an excellent school, and the Englishman instinctively comprehends its code of conduct.'

Is this belief true? The obvious people to ask are the Arabs. But during my 60 years with the Arabs I have never put the question to them direct, and I suspect that if I did they would be too polite to give me an honest answer.

GERMAN SCHOLARS AND BRITISH ADMINISTRATORS

It is probably true, with some reservations that the British know the Arabs better than any other western people do. But even that was not always the case. When I began to learn Arabic in 1944 my tutor told me at the start of my first lesson that there was no point in going on unless I could read German. That was because in those days most European scholarship on the Arab world had been produced by the Germans or in German. Indeed it was the custom before 1939 for British graduates in Arabic (and in other oriental subjects) to go on to German universities if they wished to pursue their studies seriously. Most of the standard works were by German scholars: Wellhausen, Brockelmann, Goldziher, Noldeke. Even today the essential Arabic-English dictionary for working purposes is a brilliant book by a German, Professor Wehr.

But the German approach to the Arabs in those days was largely academic. By contrast, the basis of the British relationship was practical. We had an empire and we had imperial officials, giants like Lorimer, Cox, Shakespeare, Lawrence and Philby. The Germans knew about Arabs in history. We knew about contemporary Arabs. The Germans could read and write; we could speak and listen.

But who were the British who could speak and listen to the Arabs? They were a group of imperial administrators who had been specially trained for a special job. They were certainly not the generality of the British populace. For them, if they had any acquaintance at all with the Arabs, it was usually based on brief military or clerical service during the two world wars, in which the locals they met were gully-gully men at Port Said or obsequious guides at Babylon or Baalbek. The view of the Arabs which they brought home to their families was as false and superficial as the picture they had formed of the Red Indians from the Wild West films of their childhood.

WHICH ARABS?

Even the specialist elite, from their different and deeper experience, formed a distorted view. They saw – and liked and respected – the Arabs. But which Arabs? The ones they felt affection and sympathy for were the romantic *bedouin*, the Robin Hoods of the desert, killing their last sheep to honour the guest, and the simple peasants who needed to be rescued from their rich and oppressive overlords. They had no time for the *effendis*, the students, the new graduates, the urban merchants, all of whom were in their opinion too big for their boots. This at a time when the Bedouin way of life was beginning to die and the Arab masses had started to feel their way towards freedom, independence and social progress. These expert Arabists saw the early Arab nationalists as Bolshevik upstarts. Even a deeply conservative politician like Shukry Quwatli in Syria was regarded as a danger to stability. As for Gamal Abdul Nasser, he was not, for that generation of British Arabists, the natural manifestation of a new spirit rising in the world. Anthony Eden, who held a first class degree in Arabic from Oxford, saw Nasser as a new Hitler. (Nasser's rash and dictatorial ambition did not help matters).

I do not mean to underestimate my predecessors. They were much better equipped than their counterparts in other western countries. The Americans at that time had no Arabists except a few missionaries who were considered, as missionaries usually are, to be eccentric idealists. The American Government took little interest in the Middle East until, during the Second World War, the oil companies persuaded them that they had better change their attitude. The Germans were still for the most part academics and the Nazi government relied on its anti-Jewish credentials. The French, unpopular anyway because of their policies in northwest Africa, could not compete. Even so harsh a critic of British imperialism as Edward Said says, 'It was a matter of common consensus that the French could not match the British in quality of personnel... there were no French Lawrences or Sykeses or Bells.'

SPECIALISED TRAINING
It was this quality of British personnel that supplied some justification for the idea of a special relationship. But the times were changing. It was becoming clear that the old generation of British Arabists were falling out of date. During the 1939-45 war the British Government recognised – or half recognised – the problem. They started crash courses in Arabic for the forces. They set up the Scarborough Committee which, once the war was over, established new posts, new departments, new scholarships in Arabic (and other oriental languages) in universities throughout

the land. And in 1944 they founded the Middle East Centre for Arab Studies (MECAS), at first in Jerusalem and later in the Lebanon, to train officers, government officials and businessmen not only in the Arabic language but also in Arab history, Arab society, and Arab religion. Soon there were sixty graduates a year.

Hence came a new generation of British Arabists, not so scholarly as their forebears nor so magisterial, but young men in a new world under a new government with a new attitude. And their teachers, at MECAS anyway, were for the most part Palestinians – and Palestinian *effendis* at that. I was in Shemlan in the fifties. We were all patriotic British citizens. But we were all depressed by what our government had done in Palestine and we were all shocked by the Suez crisis of 1956. We no longer dreamt of riding with the tribes on a camel raid; we were not 'crazed with the spell of far Arabia', as the poet Walter de la Mare sang. But we saw the Arabs as fellow human beings and not as imperial subjects.

I remember a day when I sat discussing the recent Suez fiasco with a group of Druze elders in the mountain village of Aitat. An old, devoutly Anglophile sheikh was lauding the British. 'Great Britain', he said, 'does not look one month ahead or one year. She looks fifty years ahead.'

I said nothing, but wished he had been right. We new Arabists were concerned for justice and equally we were concerned for our country's interests. We could see that here was a case where justice and the national interest coincided. And we could see, with dismay, that our government had made a disastrous mistake.

GOVERNMENT POLICY

That takes me from the personal relationship of British individuals with the Arabs to the realm of government policy. I have forgotten who it was who said that the British Empire was acquired in a fit of absent-mindedness. I don't suppose many of you accept that theory. But there is a grain of truth in it. Elizabeth Monroe, in her book *Britain's Moment in the Middle East*, says that after the Indian Mutiny of 1857:

> Britain was chary of taking on the management of more Orientals. Acquisition of territory on the mainland was out of

the question. The British desire and technique was to create friendly buffer states by means of influence exercised through trade treaties, loans, friendly advice and pressure by ambassadors or gunboats if necessary.

We can see this policy in Egypt, where the liberal, anti-imperialist government of Gladstone was reluctant to move in; in Aden, where what we really wanted was a coaling station and to hell with the deserts that lay behind it; and in the Gulf, where we needed safe sea-routes to India and wanted no truck with the tribal feuds on the shore. On this view there was no conspiracy, no unified purpose, only a confusion of aims and interests and a conflict between the Foreign Office and the Government of India. A typical British muddle. Some may smile sceptically at this explanation. I am more charitable.

But even if we accept that this was the British approach, there are three big weaknesses in it. First, once you are involved, however peripherally, you are constantly drawn closer. You invest in Egypt and when the investments go wrong you are pressed to move in and protect the investments. You clear the seaways in the Gulf by applying pressure to the sheikhs and sultans and then they look to you for support and for arbitration in their disputes. Or there are hopes of oil and both the oilmen and the rulers press you to define the boundaries between the states.

The second weakness is that once you have established influence over rulers you become aligned with them and, as Elizabeth Monroe said, 'Rulers run by foreigners soon lose the respect of their people.' So there is internal discontent and you are part of it.

Thirdly, in Britain – but I suspect one can find the same thing in other western states (certainly in France) – once you have established a hegemony or a protectorate there is usually a group of diehards who are attracted by the idea of empire and who resist any proposals to withdraw or compromise. Look at the so-called Suez group, led by such people as Julian Amery, which opposed Eden's efforts to reach agreement with Nasser on withdrawal from Egypt in the early fifties and which later supported his foolish invasion. Such groups find an echo even in left-wing circles, which are uneasy about being exposed to charges of 'betraying our imperial heritage'. Both left and right were able to disguise their imperialism behind a claim that we had a duty to stay and help backward peoples to develop strength and stability. Their claim is now laughed at; but once again it is not entirely comical. As I contrast the chaos and misery in the Sudan today with the stability and low-level prosperity of the British administration before 1955 I become less confident of my anti-imperialist instincts.

But that is now all in the past. In the field of government relations many things have changed. The British are no longer the leading foreign players in the Arab world. Their moment in the Middle East ended in 1956. Now they need to sell their exports. They need to buy oil, and, increasingly, non-oil imports. For their part the Arabs, too, need imports and exports and in addition they need foreign investments. Their first flush of commercial nationalism is over and foreign investors are warmly welcomed. There is no special relationship with Britain: we now have powerful foreign rivals, notably the USA and Japan. But the British and the Arabs are not masters and subjects; commercially and economically we are partners.

PALESTINE

Politically the scene is more confused. On the one hand, on the central question of Palestine there has been a big change in Britain over the past twenty years. Under Harold Wilson, and to a lesser extent, James Callaghan, the Government was strongly biased in favour of Israel. In 1978, as ambassador to Syria, I was officially rebuked for calling on the PLO representative in Damascus. Even in 1984 Margaret Thatcher refused to receive a delegation from the Arab League because it included a representative of the PLO. Observe the change since then: Yasser Arafat has been received at Downing Street and British ministers have openly criticised Israel's policies. Moreover, the British public has come to a greater understanding of the Palestinians' case. Many members of Parliament are outspoken advocates of that case. Sir Gerald Kaufman, for example, a leading Zionist, constantly attacks Israel's behaviour. CAABU flourishes. MAP flourishes. The city of Dundee is twinned with Ramallah. On the other hand, British

Government policy does not fully reflect that change. Of course our role in the Middle East is subordinate to that of the Americans; and of course we need the Americans' friendship. But we could and should be arguing for balance more vigorously and more publicly. I do not believe that we are even arguing privately. And until we are seen to be pressing harder for a settlement on Palestine Anglo-Arab governmental relations are going to remain uneasy.

IRAQ

Suez and Palestine have bedevilled Anglo-Arab relations for many years. The invasion of Iraq may do the same. The idea that outsiders could impose democracy – or any other system of government – on the most complex and disparate country in the Middle East seems to me a piece of egregious folly. The overwhelming majority of the Middle East specialists I know, on both sides of the Atlantic, agree with that view. The British tried it in the 1920s at a time when Arab nationalism was in its infancy and the physical means of resisting the foreigners was scarcely available. Writing of the insurgency in 1920 Gertrude Bell said we had been blind, and Elizabeth Monroe added: 'The cost of blindness was fighting which lasted until the spring of 1921 with a loss of some hundreds of British dead and missing and a bill of £50 million. People began to wonder whether Mesopotamia was worth such an outlay.' It is the same now, but worse.

Moreover, the idea that the arrival of democratic regimes will magically turn the Arabs into allies of the west and friends of Israel is equally absurd. The Arab street is more, not less, hostile to the west than its present rulers. Governments have to be realistic. They have to balance sentiment against pragmatic needs. They have to consider practical matters: security, the national budget, the balance of payments, the need for foreign investment, oil sales. The masses care little for all that: they are governed by emotion. And the emotion roused by recent events in Iraq has made a restless Middle East even more unstable.

AMERICAN DIPLOMACY

On a personal level things are much better. For fifty years the Foreign Office has been training six or seven officers a year in Arabic; first at MECAS, now in London and Cairo. Except occasionally in the Lebanon and the Maghrib our ambassadors always speak Arabic. No other government can match that record. The Americans have more Arabists than us, but not proportionately more. And their Arabists are handicapped, first by the system of choosing ambassadors on political or financial grounds so that Arabists often do not reach the top ranks, and secondly by the prevailing suspicion in Washington that all Arabists are anti-Israel. Often in my career Arabs have said to me: British diplomats understand us and know our history and our culture; the Americans are ignorant. I have always replied: you are wrong; the Americans have first-class Arabists; the difference is that while we are listened to, our American colleagues are distrusted.

In a relationship between two peoples the ability to speak each other's language is a powerful factor. Interpreters, however skilful, impose a barrier to intimacy. If I had fifteen minutes' conversation with King Fahd we could get through more business than my French colleague could in half an hour, and we would be more genial, more relaxed, more confidential. With the Arabs language is particularly important. No other people are so concerned with their language, so proud of it. My late friend and mentor, Sir Anthony Parsons, used to say, with only a small degree of exaggeration, that Arabs have only two subjects of conversation: Palestine and Arabic grammar. When you have just met an Arab at a dinner party and are wondering what to talk about, you should always seek his views on the adverbial accusative.

Forgive me if I digress for a moment on the Arabs' attitude to foreigners who speak Arabic. This is curiously divided. On the one hand, they are always pleased that you are making the attempt and they are astonishingly polite and flattering. When in your early stages you diffidently manage to mutter 'Good Morning', they invariably call over a friend and say 'Listen, this man speaks Arabic better than you or me.' It is completely untrue, but it is encouraging. On the other hand, they never really believe that a foreigner can truly speak Arabic. I think it is because they regard Arabic as the most subtle and complex language in the world, so difficult that only Arabs can master it. I remember an Embassy party in Beirut, given to entertain the local staff and their families. I was talking Arabic with a fair degree of fluency to one of our clerks. A lady came up and in a pause in the conversation she interrupted and said, 'Excuse me, you must be Mr Craig. My husband is a driver with the Embassy and he has told me about your Arabic. But I had no idea you were so fluent or so idiomatic. It really is wonderful.' But – and here comes the punch line – she said all this in broken French (fearing, I am sure, that I would not understand her Arabic).

The speaking of Arabic has made great strides in Britain since the days when I began. The Oxford Arabic syllabus in the forties ended in the year 1258 with the conquest of Baghdad by the Mongols. Neither history nor literature continued after that. After four years I had read much pre-Islamic poetry, most of the Koran and its commentaries and many of the great classical authors, but I could not say 'how are you?' I was, though, pretty good on the adverbial accusative. In many cases our teachers, though very erudite, were not much better. In the twenties the Oxford professor of Arabic gave a lecture in Cairo at which the Egyptians thought he was speaking English and the British thought he was speaking Arabic. The great Orientalist, A. J. Arberry, could speak no Arabic and had no interest in the modern Middle East. Now we have Arab teachers in our universities, all our graduates can speak colloquial, and we have a thriving community of thousands of Arabs in London and other cities. There are six Lebanese restaurants in Oxford. The BBC Arabic Service and the World Service have a wide audience in the Middle East and a reputation for independence and impartiality.

CONCLUSION

My conclusion is that on the personal level Anglo-Arab relations are good and healthy. At government level we are in serious trouble.

I have been critical of British policy in the Middle East over the years, starting with the Balfour Declaration of 1917, which Elizabeth Monroe described as 'one of the greatest mistakes in our imperial history'. It is only fair to add that the Arab side has not been without its faults. For the past century the world has given the Arabs a raw deal. But that is not the whole story. They have shown a sad tendency to blame their misfortunes on everyone but themselves. They have been independent states for a long time now. Yet they have not made the progress that might have been expected: not in economic development nor in science and technology nor in domestic reform. Contrast that with the performance of other states, which started from a similar level: with Malaysia, for example, or India, China or even South Korea. The Arabs have a lot of catching up to do if they are to match the achievements of their glorious history.

It is not easy to build up a partnership of equals when the gap between us in many aspects of life is growing, not reducing, and when the 22 Arab states have proved unable to settle their differences and coordinate their policies. Compared with, for example, the European Union, the Arab League has been a pretty ineffective affair. So there are faults on both sides. *Inshallah*, we can do much better in the future.

BRITAIN AND KUWAIT

Richard Muir

Kuwait is renowned throughout the region for robust and open debate, whether in the columns of its press, in the National Assembly or its famous diwanniyas. Kuwait's long relationship with the United Kingdom has been characterised by a similar frankness and openness. Many aspects have already been explored in lectures, books and articles in both Britain and Kuwait. It would be impossible to cover the ground in today's short talk. So I propose here to give some flavour of the relationship and to identify a number of trends that are still relevant today. Recent events in Iraq have been yet another reminder – if any were needed in the Middle East – that policy makers are unwise to ignore history.

ORIGINS

Kuwait's relationship with Britain has gone through several phases, each distinguished by strong personalities: from the 1899 Treaty of Friendship, through over 40 years of formal British protection for Kuwait as an independent Shaikhdom, to an informal alliance between modern states.

Kuwait's origins in the mid seventeenth century coincided with Britain's first adventures in the Gulf. There were few direct contacts until the early nineteenth century when Kuwait emerged as the leading carrier of Gulf trade and a major pearling centre. A British report of 1838 described Kuwait as, 'a clean, active town containing some 20,000 inhabitants and attracting Arab and Persian merchants from all quarters by the equity of its rule and the freedom of its trade'.

Like Britain, Kuwait's interest lay in keeping the Gulf open for trade and communication with India. As the steamship and wireless telegraph opened the Gulf to international trade British officials charted Kuwait's waters and began to see its strategic potential. In 1865 the explorer, Colonel Pelly passed through Kuwait on his way to Riyadh and reported that the Khor Abdalla waterway to the north of Kuwait could some day make a major port linked by railway through Mesopotamia to Europe.

Heightened European activity in the Gulf caused concern in Constantinople. The Ottomans saw their ramshackle Empire at risk and moved troops into Arabia. Kuwait had little option but to accept outward symbols of Ottoman authority as the price of local independence. The Shaikh of Kuwait was given the title of *qaimaqam* (local governor); there were intermittent religious prayers for the Sultan as Caliph. Yet Turkish authority was tenuous; no Turkish representatives or troops were ever in Kuwait. The British saw Turkey as the sick man of Europe; Turkish activity around Kuwait was unlikely to damage British interests. London was content to consider Kuwait, as the Captain of *HMS Sphinx* reported after a visit in 1896, 'greatly under Turkish influence.'

TREATY OF FRIENDSHIP

Several factors combined to change this view and to bring Kuwait and Britain much closer together. In 1896 Shaikh Mubarak seized control of Kuwait from his older brother. Mubarak looked first to the Turks for support. They hesitated as the Al Sabah family split and Mubarak's opponents tried a counter coup from Turkish territory. Mubarak appealed to the British, first through the Consul at Basra who reported to the Ambassador at Constantinople. The Ambassador had no wish to damage relations with the Sultan and took no action.

Mubarak then approached Colonel Meade the Political Agent across the Gulf at Bushire. This was a shrewd move. Bushire was a British Indian outpost. Meade's report caught the attention of the new Viceroy. Lord Curzon had travelled widely in Persia and spoke with authority on the Gulf. He had already warned that the Russians aimed to take Persia, reach the Gulf and establish another point of pressure there on India. There had since been talk of a Russian or of a German scheme for a railway through Ottoman territories to Baghdad and on through Basra to the Gulf – Pelly's 1865 vision but implemented by a rival power. The prospect of Turkey allowing Russia or Germany through Mesopotamia to the top of the Gulf rang alarm bells in India. London was less concerned but agreed that an attempt should be made to secure Mubarak's loyalty.

In 1899 Meade was instructed to cross secretly to Kuwait and to seek out Mubarak. As he left Bushire Meade gave out that he was off on a hunting expedition but his cover was blown at Kuwait where he found a Turkish cruiser anchored in the bay. Meade waited for the Turks to leave and then, as instructed, urged Mubarak to sign an exclusive agreement with Britain. This required Mubarak to consult Britain before letting any other power, including Turkey, into Kuwait. In return Britain offered cash payment. Mubarak demanded more; he needed British protection against the Turks. Meade had no authority for anything of the kind but went beyond his instructions and signed a side letter with an assurance of British 'good offices'. The Turks soon found out about this secret Treaty and in 1901 gave Mubarak an ultimatum to accept Turkish troops or go into exile. Encouraged by Curzon, Meade sent a gunboat to Kuwait, honouring his commitment and saving Mubarak from the Turks.

In 1904 Curzon made a long planned visit to the Gulf to reinforce Britain's position. He would 'visit Arab shaikhs to testify to the paramount political and commercial ascendancy that is exercised by the Government of Britain in these waters'. Curzon took a flotilla of eight ships led by the four-funnel battle cruiser *HMS Argonaut*, diverted for the occasion from the Far Eastern fleet; a more impressive display of imperial power than any rival could manage. Shaikh Mubarak met Curzon as he landed, as did a specially imported carriage and a 'shouting galloping crowd, firing… and careering in every direction'. The two men hit it off; Curzon rated Mubarak 'by far the most masculine and vigorous personality that I have encountered in the Gulf... a very acute intelligence and a character which justified his general reputation for cunning'. Curzon nevertheless concluded that Mubarak would remain loyal to Britain; Britain should open a political agency in

Kuwait, even if London would still not commit to formal protection.

The Turks objected and London hesitated for a year, reawakening Mubarak's scepticism about the British commitment. But the Indian Political Service persisted and the Agency opened in 1905, exactly 100 years ago, with the arrival of Colonel Knox and a building, still there and now handsomely restored, on Kuwait's waterfront. Although Mubarak still trusted no one and kept his lines open to Turkey, Russia and Germany he granted Britain a series of exclusive concessions, reinforcing Britain's position at the top of the Gulf. Timely appearances by British gunboats helped maintain Mubarak's autonomy.

In the meantime Britain and Turkey clarified their positions in the Gulf, reaching agreement in 1913. This was not good news for Mubarak. Turkey had dropped ambitions to Bahrain and Qatar and lost Qatif to Ibn Saud but insisted that Kuwait remain nominally within the Turkish Empire and for the first time accept an official Turkish representative. Mubarak was infuriated. But the deal in fact gave him much of what he needed: Turkish recognition of his autonomy and new fixed borders. These were defined with a red line taking in Wahba and Bubiyan islands on the east side of the Khor Abdalla. A large swathe of territory to the south and west of Kuwait was defined in green; here British officials had found the tribes 'voluntarily or under compulsion owe allegiance to the Shaikh'.

PROTECTION TREATY

This Anglo-Turkish agreement collapsed with the outbreak of the First World War. Turkey sided with Germany and Britain finally gave Mubarak the formal treaty of protection he had been after since 1898. Mubarak died in 1915 'half happy with Britain, half scared of Turkey'.

By 1918 the Turkish Empire in Arabia had been swept away. The peacemakers at Versailles drew new frontiers. Britain and France took over the former Turkish territories and created new countries with League of Nations mandates. Britain was no longer a distant power but a regional player with forces on the ground in

Palestine, Transjordan and Iraq. Whitehall now had a close interest in the inner workings of Arabia. Kuwait had become an important buffer against the rising ambitions of Ibn Saud and an essential foothold at the top of the Gulf should Iraq go wrong.

So when the Ikhwan, a fundamentalist tribal force loyal to Ibn Saud, invaded Kuwaiti territory in 1920 London took notice. As the tribesmen reached the hastily strengthened walls of Kuwait City and threatened the nearby fort at Jahra British warships, armoured cars and aircraft moved in to assist Mubarak's beleaguered successor Shaikh Salem. It took the combined forces and a novel use of aircraft to shift the camel mounted Ikhwan out of Kuwaiti territory.

Properly agreed borders were urgently needed if the situation was to be stabilised. Percy Cox, an experienced Gulf hand now High Commissioner in Baghdad, took on the job. Cox and Ibn Saud met in 1922 at Uqair on the Saudi coast opposite Bahrain. Cox heard out Ibn Saud's demands for territory up to the Euphrates then took out his red pencil and drew lines on the map. He marked the Iraq/ Saudi border, confirmed the 1913 Anglo-Turkish red line between Iraq and Kuwait including Warba and Bubiyan islands, but then allocated to Ibn Saud a lot of 'green line' desert south of Kuwait where Salem had lost control. Salem had died the previous year; his successor, Ahmed remained bitter for the rest of his life at this outcome. But it gave Kuwait clear and defensible borders and provided the basis for a solid British defence of Kuwait when the Ikhwan again threatened to overrun the Shaikdom in 1928.

OIL

It was only as the Ikhwan threat receded that oil became a major factor in Kuwait/British relations. Mubarak had agreed in 1912 to give Britain first refusal on any oil concession. But the geologists found no evidence of oil. The conventional wisdom was that the deposits ran from Mosul to the Persian side of the Gulf and that none lay under Arabia. British companies, short of cash in the years after the First World War, therefore concentrated on Iraq and Persia.

A maverick New Zealander, Frank Holmes, challenged this

wisdom. By 1929 he had secured a concession in Bahrain and moved on to Kuwait. His arrival and connections with Gulf Oil of California alarmed the new British Political Agent in Kuwait, Harold Dickson.

Dickson believed that Kuwait had oil; he was an inveterate explorer and had seen the seepages in the desert. He was also persistent and determined that Britain not America should secure the Kuwait concession. Dickson persuaded London to stall Holmes' approaches and urged the Anglo-Persian Oil Company (APOC) to open negotiations with Shaikh Ahmed. Holmes and his American principles mounted diplomatic pressure through Washington. In 1932 APOC, pushed now from London as well as by Dickson and encouraged by discoveries in Bahrain, agreed to a joint approach with Gulf Oil and formed the 50/50 Kuwait Oil Company (KOC). Shaikh Ahmed could no longer play the British against the Americans but negotiated on for another two years before signing a concession agreement with KOC on the dining table at the British Political Agency. At the time Kuwait was destitute; the war and the depression had damaged trade; the pearling industry had collapsed and the prospects of finding oil still looked remote. Shaikh Ahmed had played a canny hand.

Although the United States was now a significant economic player in the region Britain remained the only military power and was still the essential guarantor of Kuwait's security. As a symbol of commitment – perhaps reinforced by the prospect of oil – the British Government urged on by Dickson built a new agency on land Shaikh Ahmed provided near his Dasman Palace.

With Iraqi independence in 1932 the Kuwait/Iraq border began to give trouble, as increasingly did Iraqi claims to Kuwait as a former province of the Ottoman Empire. Britain worried that having escaped absorption by Saudi Arabia, Kuwait now faced absorption by Iraq. British officials took a firm line; there had never been any question of Turkish sovereignty over Kuwait; Iraqi claims had no basis. The Iraqis backed off on sovereignty but continued throughout the Second World War to contest Kuwaiti ownership of Warba and Bubiyan islands, demanding control of both banks of the Khor Abdalla waterway between Um Qasr and the sea.

The war delayed oil development but soon after it ended Kuwait exported its first tanker of oil in June 1946 on BP's *British Fusilier*. Several months later India reached independence. The rationale for British interest in Kuwait began to shift. As the route to India lost significance Kuwait's oil and sterling revenues became central to the British economy. By the mid 1950s Kuwait was supplying more than half Britain's oil and Kuwaiti revenues were propping up the fragile sterling area. Kuwait's stability and security as an oil producer were a vital British interest. Whitehall worried and began to look more closely at Kuwait's internal affairs. Could Kuwait's government cope as the oil wealth poured in and the economy boomed; were the Al Sabah up to the job? Should they not have British financial advisers? The Foreign Office saw the dangers of getting mixed up in Kuwait's internal affairs; its officials argued in 1955: 'Our position in Kuwait must be flexible and we must take care not to jeopardise the position and influence we have got by seeking too brashly to extend them and to force advice down the Kuwaitis' throats'; a point which has resonance today.

Suez in 1956 marked the beginning of the end for Britain's moment as a power in the Middle East. In 1958 Qassim and the Iraqi military overthrew the Hashemite Government Britain had installed in Iraq. Arab nationalism fanned by Nasser and *Sawt Al Arab* radio, swept through the region. Reformist voices in Kuwait demanded a distancing from Britain, full independence, UN and Arab League membership. The Ruler, now Shaikh Abdulla Salim, and many British officials recognised the need to move on. Britain accepted that Kuwait should begin to diversify its overseas investments through the new Kuwait Fund and negotiate concessions with oil companies without reference to the British Government. In 1961 Britain agreed to wind up the formal 1914 protection agreement, with an understanding that Britain would still if necessary come to Kuwait's assistance. For Britain oil remained crucial; as Edward Heath then Lord Privy Seal put it: 'Access to Kuwait's oil resources on the best financial terms possible remain vital interests for the United Kingdom and these would be endangered should Kuwait lose her independence'. For their part the Kuwaitis were clear that intervention should only take place if they requested it.

INTERNATIONALISATION

They soon did. Weeks after the protection agreement ended Qasim reopened the Iraqi claim to Kuwait as part of the Province of Basra. Both Britain and Kuwait moved fast. The Amir invited British troops back; the Macmillan Government rushed in 7,000 men but, recognising that times had changed, supported the Kuwaiti invitation to an Arab force and its application to the Arab League. The new reality was that the Al Sabah needed regional allies – in this case Nasser's Egypt – as well as Britain, now a declining but still dominant power in the Gulf. As Robert Walmsley of the Arabian Department minuted: 'mentally it is difficult, but politically it is necessary (for Britain) to stop thinking of Kuwait as a 'Gulf Shaikhdom', and to treat it as the foreign and friendly Arab power which it is'.

By 1968 the 1961 understanding on British military support for Kuwait had also been wound up by mutual agreement as Britain decided to withdraw all forces from the Gulf. This left a power vacuum. America, burnt by experience in Vietnam rejected the request of Amir Shaikh Sabah Salim on his first visit as Amir to Washington to take on Britain's role. It was in fact twenty years before America did so with agreement at the end of the Iran/Iraq war in 1988 to reflag and protect tankers heading for Kuwait.

Saddam underestimated this new American commitment when he invaded Kuwait in August 1990. And it was a mistake too to think that Britain had left the Gulf. By 1990 there were more British expatriates in Kuwait and the other Gulf states than at any time in history. Britain remained influential in the region as well as at the UN and behind the scenes in Washington. Margaret Thatcher's 'don't go wobbly George' had impact, driven by visceral British opposition to an attempt by an aggressive dictator to swallow up a smaller and weaker state as well as by long friendship with Kuwait. The close ties came out in many ways; at the Bank of England the Governor unhesitatingly moved Kuwait assets out of Saddam's reach and gave his Kuwaiti counterpart and the exiled Government immediate access to all the funds they needed.

Kuwait's security once again depended on lining up an international coalition alongside the western power. Crucial to this were the 1990 UN Security Council Resolutions. They enabled Kuwait to accept British and American assistance as part of a legal international effort without damage to its credentials as an independent Arab state.

CONCLUSIONS

For much of the last century Britain and Kuwait relied heavily on each other. Mubarak was sceptical of the British commitment. But it saved him in 1901 and was to save Kuwait three more times under the treaties of protection, in 1920, 1928 and 1961. For Britain, Kuwait was at first a vital asset to Empire and then an equally vital provider of oil and financial support. The shared experience shaped Kuwait's history. The relationship, which continues today, might be termed one of strategic affinity. It was there in 1990-91 when Britain came again to Kuwait's defence. It was there too when Britain went into Iraq in April 2003. For Kuwait, Britain remains a dependable ally. For Britain, that continues to entail responsibilities to Kuwait.

I would like to end with some specifics. First, acceptance on the British side that Kuwait, like our other friends in the Arab world must go on making its own choices. Decisions on international relations, on major economic issues such as OPEC production and on domestic issues such as votes for women, the introduction of political parties and conditions for foreign investors and the re-entry of international oil companies must be for Kuwait to take for itself. That does not mean that we should not have views and express them – robustly when necessary. But in doing so we should speak from knowledge of the shared past, of what will and what will not work.

Second, Britain still has an important role to play in the security of the Gulf and of Kuwait in particular. The issue of Iraq is not yet played out. Britain has a deep involvement there and owes it to Kuwait to ensure that the border settlement reached under the Security Council in 1993, endorsing the British lines drawn in 1913 and in the 1920s, remains intact. Britain has the historic perspective to provide this assurance.

Third, Kuwait has recognised the need to move faster in

diversifying and developing its economy. Britain can assist in many ways. It is a source of particular pleasure to me, and I am sure it would be to David Gore Booth, ever the Commercial diplomat, that Britain is involved in developing Kuwait's major new port for the region on Bubiyan Island, the site identified by Pelly 140 years ago, and a key to future regional cooperation.

BRITAIN AND BAHRAIN

Roger Tomkys

It is tempting for me to regard Anglo-Bahraini relations as uniquely close and special, since is the only Gulf state in which I have lived for a long period. Of course throughout the region there were strong personal and official links. In Bahrain, however, the intensity of the symbiosis goes back a long way. I will not start as the full story should with nineteenth century Treaties and the arrival of Political Agents reporting to the Residency in Bushire and the Indian Government in Bombay, but with the appointment of Charles Belgrave in the early twenties as Adviser to Sheikh Hamad. It was a key moment because it came at a time of communal troubles in Bahrain leading to intervention, however indirect, by the Political Agency in the internal affairs of the country.

A VALUABLE INFRASTRUCTURE

Belgrave in his three and a half decades of service to successive rulers played a key part, not underestimated in his own memoirs, published as *A Personal Column*, in the building of modern Bahrain. Law and order, the legal structure of the sheikhdom, education for both men and women, the regulation of the pearling industry and transition to the oil and service economy all owed much to Belgrave and his service to the ruling family. Surely it was this fundamental structure that made Bahrain the natural location for the Political Residency when Britian moved from Bushire and transferred responsibility from Delhi and Bombay after the Second World War to the Arab side of the Gulf at the outset of the oil age.

Belgrave's major contribution was crucial and his commitment to his employers and the interests of Bahrain absolute. Yet characteristically it was not without friction and this illustrates for me another aspect of the complex relationship of our two countries. Belgrave kept a diary to which he confided his more private thoughts, not without exasperation from time to time with his employers. Although what he wrote was always imbued with close affection and respect it was understandable that when the diaries came to light after Charles' death the Ruler and his advisers should have regarded their publication as unacceptable. The moral that I draw from this story is simple: observers have often commented on the exceptional and close British-Bahraini relationship; successive British Ambassadors and British residents in other capacities have enjoyed the great benefits of this closeness; I have done so myself and I greatly treasure the memory of Sheikh Isa bin Salman as Ruler and, I dare say, friend. But what outside observers have often missed is that the closeness of the friendship was always built on the principle of mutual respect and more especially, the independence of Bahrain and the authority of its Ruler.

If the legacy of cooperation, with Belgrave an important medium, made Bahrain the natural site for the post war Political Residency, it also made Bahrain with an early developed infrastructure, an educated population, early industrialisation based on the limited oil discovered at Jebal Dukhan, together with a strong legal framework and an established merchant community, the natural communications and services centre for the Gulf in the modern era.

In the early eighties, just after the Iranian revolution and a few years after the second oil shock of the 1970s, Bahrain was in rapid economic transition. Over the decades a mix of conservatism and initiative had laid the foundation. The Ruler's direct benevolence and steadfast principles, together with his accessibility, human warmth and natural generosity held the country together. There was an educated and hardworking Bahraini workforce able to man the growing oil, aluminium, shipbuilding and port facilities; and all concerned know that it was politically as well as economically essential that there should be employment, education, social and health services for all Bahraini nationals. The Prime Minister Sheikh Khalifa with a group of the young technocratic Ministers –

Yusuf Shirawi, Ali Fakhro, Tariq Almoayed and many others, provided the energy, initiative and drive. Sheikh Mohammed bin Mubarak and Sheikh Mohammed bin Khalifa though young had long experience as Foreign Minister and at the Interior respectively, and Sheikh Hamed supported closely by Sheikh Khalifa bin Ahmed commanded the small but disciplined Defence Force. On the economic and commercial side the large, senior and experienced merchant community worked closely with government in the development of the hotel industry, Alba, Gulf Air, the financial section, the petrochemical, telecommunication and maritime businesses. It was an old established partnership; the roles were distinct and although the dividing lines were not rigid, everyone knew that a balance had to be respected. All this was underpinned not, indeed, by Westminster-style democracy, but by strong lines of more traditional accountability and, Sheikh Isa's personal gift, accessibility within a working civil society.

There was, however, an additional dimension, the continuity of the British connection. For the historic reasons to which I have already alluded, the British presence was by for the most pervasive of all Western influences and Sheikh Isa regarded this as the natural law of things. With this was associated the presence in Bahrain of the most senior of British expatriate representatives in the Gulf, in the Standard and Chartered Bank, for British Airways, at Gray Mackenzie, for Africa and Eastern and for Cable and Wireless and so forth. These were men who had made much of their lives in the Gulf and much of the industrialisation of Bahrain was built up in partnership with them. For someone like Yusuf Shirawi it was as natural to set up between Bahraini merchants and British partners a joint venture underpinned by his close friendships with the British businessmen concerned as it had been for him to cut deals with Tony Parsons and other British Political Agents and, after 1971, Ambassadors.

AN INTERNATIONAL BANKING CENTRE
This takes me to the new-style international banking sector. This had developed swiftly at the end of the seventies to a point, at my arrival in 1981, when it was still growing rapidly and was no longer

an infant sector at risk. Its establishment with Abdullah Seif as first Governor of the Bahrain Monetary Agency (BMA), under the careful guidance of Sayyid Mahmood's successor at Finance, Ibrahim Abdul Karim, gave Bahrain an internationally regulated environment to which major banks and other service providers could come with confidence. This confidence was assured not least by the guidance and support provided largely by the Bank of England through the agency of Alan Moore as advisor. When I accompanied Abdulla Seif and Ibrahim Abul Karim to London on an official visit in 1982 or 1983, two things were clear in meetings with the Chancellor, with the Governor of the Bank of England and other City figures: first that the Bank of England and the British Government accepted responsibility for supporting Bahrain; and second that the Bahrain side while wholly independent looked to London for that advice and support.

My next remarks are to update that picture. In the last few years I have once again, after a substantial interval, seen the Bahrain services sector at fairly close quarters. There is both continuity and inevitable change. On the one hand the British presence and influence though still strong are no longer dominant. The almost pro-consular, long term British resident 'great and good' have few contemporary equals. British financial and trading interests are now overshadowed by a fully international presence. In part this must reflect the reality: twenty-five years on the quasi-imperial past is ancient history and the United States is the economic as well as military superpower. In part, I believe it reflects a well judged Bahraini understanding that the country no longer needs a special relationship, whatever the ties of affection that bind Britain and Bahrain together. Thus, for me, seeing Bahraini Ministers and BMA Governors operate in the world of the twenty-first century, the time for any kind of tutelage or the need for guidance is wholly absent.

On the other hand, the legacy, it seems to me of past cooperation is as powerful as ever. I have emphasised the British contribution to the establishment of a sound legal and administrative framework essential to the building and the prosperity of an international finance, commerce and services sector, going hand in hand with the working of a civil society to which all the nationals of the country owe allegiance and within which expatriates of all origins and all walks of life can feel confidence in the rule of law. Bahrain has advanced enormously in the years since I was Ambassador and as a British friend of Bahrain I feel pride that although the British contribution today is relatively reduced, the systems which British advisers, diplomats, ex-businessmen and bankers helped to put in place in the past are ever more important.

CONCLUSIONS

In many respects Bahrain has explored in advance of its Gulf neighbours the possibilities of earning its way in the world and providing productive service and industrial employment for its nationals without over reliance on the rent inherent in crude oil production. It is no longer unique in its diversification, no longer the sole financial centre. If a new location on the Arab side of the Gulf were needed for a latter-day British Political Residency relocated from Bushire, there would be other contenders, whether through the enormous wealth creating power of huge oil and gas reserves or because of the rapid development of new service sectors. I continue, however, to be convinced that the mix of experience and far sighted early development that marked Bahrain will continue to give it an edge for international and regional groups in all sectors which depend on good commercial law, equitable and far sighted regulation, and an environment in which expatriates and their families as well as Bahrainis and GCC nationals can live and work in harmony.

I am glad that Britain made a substantial contribution over many decades to this Bahraini achievement.

BRITAIN AND QATAR

Graham Boyce

The history of Qatar's relations with Britain is short, rather less than 150 years. During that time, British decisions have often had a profound effect on the development of Qatar as a State, while the British, for much of this history, seem to have had very little regard for what the interests of Qatar might be. In the nineteenth century Qatar was just seen as an unruly haven for piracy which upset British plans for the Gulf to be a peaceful waterway which did not disturb British interests in India. Britain had long had a strategic interest in Persia, and up to as late as 1946, the main British diplomatic presence in the Gulf was the Political Residency in Bushire. For much of the last century, British interests on the southern side of the Gulf focussed on Bahrain, and decisions affecting Qatar were always seen through that prism. This sense of the British only taking notice of Qatar when it obtruded into Britain's other interests in the area, persisted for a surprising length of time. Even now, Qatar's strategic importance as a key base for US forces in the region, its immense resources of gas and its pioneering reform programme still do not excite the sort of attention in London that either Britain's supporters or competitors might expect. For their part, the Qataris tend to interpret Britain's careless disregard as deliberate, with conspiracy theories to explain every British action, which makes for something of a roller coaster relationship. But what is remarkable is that despite official misunderstanding and over complication of the issues that do arise between the two countries, personal relations can still be very warm, and the prospects for a fully mature relationship between the two countries is probably better now than they have ever been in the past.

PIRACY AND REPRISALS

Britain's interest in the Gulf first arose through its commercial rivalry with the Portuguese and the Dutch over commercial interests in India. So the first British presence to have an impact on the southern sheikhdoms of the Gulf was not the British government but the British East India Company. As maritime trade started to grow, so too did piracy, and it was piracy that first brought Qatar to British attention in the nineteenth century. In 1820, the East India ship *Vestal* destroyed Doha by fire for breaching an agreement a year earlier with a number of Gulf Sheiks not to harbour pirates. This harsh action took the Qataris by surprise: they had not been party to the agreements and knew nothing of them. At that time, the British assumed that the leaderless Qataris were just an adjunct of Bahrain. Qatar as a single political force did not really emerge until Mohammed Al Thani asserted his authority over the tribes of the Qatar peninsula in the 1850s, which is when the story of Qatar's relations with Britain really begins.

1850 - 1918

The movement of tribes along the Arabian littoral was active and complex during the eighteenth and nineteenth centuries. By the mid nineteenth century, the Al Khalifah were well established, via a period in Qatar, as rulers in Bahrain. In 1842 the Qataris became involved in the conflict between the co-rulers of Bahrain, Sheikh Abdullah bin Khalifah and his great nephew Sheikh Mohammed. Sheikh Mohammed was expelled that year, settling in Qatar, but overthrew Sheikh Abdullah the following year with Qatari help. Despite this help, relations turned sour in 1867, with a series of battles between the two Sheikdoms in the following year. Events appeared to be getting out of hand and the British intervened, blaming the Bahrainis for the trouble. It was at this stage that the first official contact between Britain and Qatar took place, when Colonel Pelly met Sheikh Mohammed Al Thani in Qatar. When Colonel Pelly later arrived in Bahrain with three warships, Sheikh Mohammed fled to Qatar. Sheikh Ali Al Khalifah then took over power in Bahrain, and signed a grovelling letter paying a fine for

Sheikh Mohammed's acts of piracy and promising to keep the peace. On 11 September 1868, a further letter was signed by Sheikh Mohamed al Thani, in which he too promised to keep the peace and refer all disputes to the British Resident. This was an important milestone. Following that first meeting with Pelly the previous year, it confirmed the equal status of Bahrain and Qatar and the authority of the two Rulers over their respective territories.

KEEPING THE PEACE

At this stage, there was no question of Britain seeking to exert any internal control in either Sheikhdom. The sole British interest was in keeping the peace so that the free flow of trade should not be interrupted. At this stage too, the British were well aware that there was another actor on stage who did claim the right to dictate to the Sheikhs on internal matters. The Ottoman Empire already exercised control over large tracts of the Arabian side of the Gulf and sought to extend its influence further. In 1871, Qatar was offered the protection of the Ottoman Empire and the next year a garrison of Ottoman troops was established at al-Bida. At this time, the British were concerned to make sure that the Ottomans made no claims to Bahrain, but seemed untroubled by the Ottoman presence in Qatar. The British had a continuing concern about piracy emanating from Qatar under Sheikh Jassim. The orders of the British Government in 1882 to the Political Resident were that while Qatar had accepted the position of a dependent of an Ottoman dependent, Qatar should defer to the government of India on matters affecting the peace of the seas. The British will to intervene on these matters was well illustrated in 1895. When Sheikh Jassim allowed the Al bin Ali tribe to settle at Zubarah after a dispute with the Al Khalifah, and to plot with the Ottomans to attack Bahrain, this threatened not just the maritime peace, but also Britain's treaty commitment to Bahrain. A British warship destroyed 44 boats apparently assembled to attack Bahrain, and Sheikh Jassim surrendered and expelled the Al bin Ali.

Apart from the Ottomans, other powers were becoming more active in the region as the century drew to a close. As a result, Britain drew up a series of Exclusive Agreements with almost all the other rulers in the region except Qatar. Sheikh Jassim sought one too in 1891, but the British rejected his proposal on the grounds that the Ottoman Sultan would not agree. That Sheikh Jassim sought such an agreement with the British was a sign that his relations with the Ottomans were not always smooth. As the events of 1895 showed, the British too were becoming keener to define the extent of British and Ottoman control over the region. A series of negotiations lead to the Anglo-Ottoman Convention, signed in 1913. Although it was never ratified, the key points for Qatar were regarded as binding in other treaties. These were the renunciation of Ottoman claims to the Qatar peninsula, and the British undertaking to ensure that Bahrain did not interfere in Qatar's internal affairs. However, the final departure of the tiny Ottoman garrison did not take place until 1916, when a British warship arrived at Doha and the garrison slipped uneventfully away.

These events finally led to an exclusive agreement between Qatar and Britain, similar to that agreed with the other Sheikhs in the region in 1892. It was signed in 1916 and ratified on 23 March 1918. In exchange for protection, the Sheikh agreed not to receive the agents of other powers or to grant any concessions without British consent.

THE FIRST OIL CONCESSIONS

Between the two world wars, Qatar remained under the firm control of the Al Thani family, with little British interference. This was probably due to the fact that Britain's strategic interest still focussed on Bahrain. As a result, there was no permanent British representation in Qatar until 1949: until that time the Political Agent in Bahrain was responsible for reporting on Qatar. However, there was still interaction. 1935 saw the first mention of Qatar in the British press. It also saw the next major step in the relationship between the two countries. The Ruler, Sheikh Abdullah, had long been seeking improvements in his status. At that time, there were several things the British wanted from Qatar. Britain had been slow to see the prospects for oil in the Gulf. Even though they were still doubtful that commercial quantities of oil would be found in places like Qatar, they wanted to be sure that they could dictate where oil concessions should go. They also wanted landing rights and an airfield in Qatar as part of their strategic route to India. And finally, they realised that the 1916 Agreement was personal to Sheikh Jassim: to maintain Britain's strategic influence, a new agreement would be needed. Sheikh Abdullah for his part was under pressure because of a border dispute with Saudi Arabia and needed his protection by Britain clearly defined. He was never told of the potential value of the oil concessions, but still bargained hard for an agreement giving him all he wanted, including official British recognition of his son Hamad as his heir. In return, he granted the British request to build an airfield in Qatar and also gave an oil concession to the British group which was to become Petroleum Development (Qatar). Although the concession was granted then, drilling did not start for another three years, and oil was found in 1939. The outbreak of war led the British authorities to order the wells to be plugged (even at that stage there was little sign of their significance), and so it was not until December 1949 that the first shipment of oil finally left the country.

For the British, oil concessions were becoming an increasingly important issue. It was because of the need to grant further concessions in the offshore areas between Qatar and Bahrain that the British made their decisions delineating the frontiers round the shoals and islands between the two countries. That history is now well documented as a result of the exhaustive hearings before the International Court of Justice (ICJ), whose ruling in 2001 finally brought an end to a dispute which had lasted over 60 years. For Qataris, the British letters of 11 July 1939 (further reinforced by letters in 1947) granting the Hawar islands to Bahrain were wholly unacceptable. They protested against this decision at the time, and at every available opportunity thereafter. The background to the decision was in a large part shaped by Britain's relations with Bahrain. For the Al Khalifah, the ruined town of Zubarah in the west of Qatar was still part of their territory, a matter more of history and local tribal allegiances than of any fact of control or geography. But when in the late 1930s they repeatedly pressed this claim, the British were firm in supporting Qatar. When the maritime border came up for delineation and the Al Khalifah claimed the Hawar Islands with the same vigour that they showed over Zubarah, it seems that the Political Resident had little stomach for another row with the Al Khalifah and awarded the disputed territory to Bahrain. He gave the Qataris the opportunity to make a counter claim, but they lacked the legal and diplomatic expertise available to the Bahrainis and were unable to change the Resident's mind. Interestingly, many British officials at the time thought that this decision was wrong, and the succeeding Resident also thought a mistake had been made. But it seems that, having made this decision, the British were not prepared to change their minds, in view of the greater importance they attached at that time to their relations with Bahrain. The majority judgement of the ICJ upholding Bahrain's claim to the Hawar islands (but rejecting other of their claims), was heavily influenced by that 1939 letter and the fact that under the treaties of protection, Britain had had the right to decide on these frontiers, and the merits of their decision at that time were therefore of secondary importance.

The discovery of oil altered the nature of the relationship with Qatar. Oil revenue, however increased quite slowly in Qatar and the boom seen in other oil producing countries in the region crept up on Qatar more gradually. The presence of British oil workers in the country, together with a permanent Political Agent after 1949 meant much closer links than ever before. Politically, though, Qatar remained on the margins for Britain. Bahrain's strategic importance was further enhanced when the Political Resident, the most senior British official in the region, transferred from Bushire to Bahrain in 1946.

THE BRITISH WITHDRAWAL IN 1971

Britain's limited interest in Qatar was matched in Qatar by a growing sense of identity with the Arab Nationalism which was sweeping the region. At the same time Britain's empire was rapidly being dismantled as the UK economy resolutely continued to go downhill. In the late 1960s the British Labour Government decided to withdraw from the Gulf completely. The driving force behind this decision was the series of financial crises the Britain was facing, notably the devaluation of Sterling in 1967. The withdrawal was not sought by the smaller Sheikdoms, who, despite any misgivings about links with a fading imperial power, were more fearful of being left unprotected against an assertive Iran. Britain succeeded in ensuring Bahrain's independence, when Iran renounced its claim, but the success of this long-standing objective of British policy in the region also undermined the prospects for Britain's efforts to meld the nine smaller emirates into a single State. In 1968 a Federation of Arab States was announced, in which Qatar would have had a prominent role. But late in the negotiations to complete a constitution, Bahrain opted for an independent existence and Qatar followed suit. So it was that on 3 September 1971, Qatar proclaimed full independence from Britain and the last British Political Agent metamorphosed into the first British Ambassador.

POLITICAL CHANGE IN 1972 AND 1995

Independence was soon followed by political change. In 1972, Sheikh Ahmad was deposed in a peaceful coup by Sheikh Khalifah bin Hamad, a change viewed positively by the British, who had long been concerned by Sheikh Ahmad's acquisitive approach to the country's oil revenue. This pattern was repeated when Sheikh Hamad bin Khalifah overthrew his father in 1995. Sheikh Khalifah had overseen the founding of Qatar as a modern state and had been an effective ruler. But he became increasingly unwilling either to take the decisions necessary to accelerate the economic and political development of the country, or delegate them to his son. It was frustration at the slow pace of change that drove Sheikh Hamad and the younger Sheikhs to take action. This change too was quickly welcomed by the British, who saw in Sheikh Hamad the kind of progressive and energetic leader needed if small states like Qatar were going to adapt to a changing world and flourish.

Although Qatar was now an independent state, the legacy of the old relationship lingered. The British rather took Qatar for granted as a friendly presence in the region, both at the political level and in the commercial world, where this neglect of Qatari interests saw not only the departure of British (or Anglo-Dutch) oil companies, but the rapid erosion of the favourable trading position the British had previously enjoyed. For Qataris, the issue was more complex. Their protectorate status had not involved colonial rule in the way that other parts of the British Empire had experienced and there had been no struggle for independence. They could find fault with Britain (particularly over the legacy of the border with Bahrain), and they grumbled about the British, but there were no open disputes.

A 'NEW AND VERY DISTINCT IDENTITY'

Since 1995, Qatar has started to develop a new and very distinct identity. This is giving the country a new sense of self confidence, to the extent that it is now ready to treat Britain as a key partner in the country's future development, provided that the British recognise the changes that are happening and are prepared to give Qatar the level of attention it seeks.

These changes are in three areas: political, economic and social. They all derive from the vision for the country that the current Amir has developed. That vision is one which looks beyond the huge windfall which sitting on the world's largest gas field is now providing Qatar. A central feature of the long-term plan is to equip the people of Qatar to become a successful society even without the oil and gas. This involves educating the people to international standards so that they can all become contributing members of society; it means not being tied to political ideologies which might prevent Qatar from developing ties which will benefit the country, or economic ideologies which might hold back the development of the economy. And all this while trying to preserve the traditional character of Qatari society and its religious foundations. Although the Qataris profess themselves to be Wahhabis, their society is moving in ways unthinkable to the more exclusive Wahhabi society over the border in Saudi Arabia.

AL JAZEERA AND THE US BASE: A NEW PRAGMATISM

The politics of Qatar is characterised by the seeming paradox of hosting a major US base and also being the founder and home of the first Arab satellite news station Al Jazeera, seen by many Americans as directly challenging and undermining their policies in the Middle East. The driving force beyond Qatari politics is pragmatism, backed by a growing self-confidence in international politics. Earlier rulers were driven more by what was in the best interests of the Al Thani, or by a reluctance to get out of step with their Arab neighbours so this has been a profound change. The pragmatism and realism, however also have foundations in idealism. Qatar subscribes to the ideals of Islam and Arabism, but has no patience with the empty rhetoric which often surrounds them. So Qatar can be the first Arab State to give significant financial help to Israeli Arabs, and has no qualms about talking about trade with Israel either. The Amir has spoken in public about the need for the Arab world to stop blaming Israel or the west for their poor performance, and to set about putting their world in order by themselves. Qatar is also impatient with the poor example Arab autocracies present to the rest of the world. So Qatar worked hard, for example to encourage Iraq to comply with Security Council resolutions to prevent an American attack in 2003. But when Saddam Hussein seemed to continue to play games with the Security Council, Qatar was prepared to offer base facilities to the US. It will be interesting to see how this pragmatism plays out as Qatar assumes its seat on the Security Council in 2006. Thirty years ago, the thought that Qatar would be on the Security Council was unimaginable. That it will not only be there, but that it will be a voice to be listened to, is a measure of the political progress Qatar has made.

Opening Qatar to US bases and investment has been more than balanced by Qatar's unflinching support for Al Jazeera, however exasperating the Americans (and many others) find its outspoken style. The Amir genuinely believes in freedom of speech – one of his first acts as Amir was to abolish the Ministry of Information, the tool in other countries in the region for the exercise of censorship. Al Jazeera meanwhile has become better known than Qatar itself. It has caused one of the biggest shifts in the Arab political scene in the last half century, by destroying the monopoly over news enjoyed by authoritarian regimes across the Arab world. Not only has this opened the eyes of the Arab viewers to the unauthorised story, it has also given them a new self-confidence, to see an Arab channel compete professionally with the best in the world. Perhaps the highest accolade is the BBC decision to launch a new Arab satellite channel, specifically to compete with Al Jazeera.

THE NEW CONSTITUTION

In domestic politics too, the new constitution, ratified in 2004, is a model of pragmatism. It offers no headlong rush to a democratically elected government, but offers further steps along that road first trodden with municipal elections, complete with full rights for women. But it also aspires to high ideals. There are provisions for equality before the law (it has already been shown that members of the ruling family are not above the law), independence of the judiciary, the rights of women and freedom of worship. All this has come about without external pressure, and at a pace which the Government judges that Qatar's traditional and tribal society can handle. The elections expected in 2006 will start to put this new process to the test.

Similar principles apply in development of the economy. While Qatar's neighbours agonise about keeping sovereignty and control over their natural resources, Qatar has leaped ahead by opening the door to international companies to help develop its huge gas resources. Qatar is poised to become the world's largest exporter of Liquefied Natural Gas and will be the world's largest producer of the new gas-to-liquids technologies. Typically pragmatic was their dealing with Shell. Shell had left Qatar in the 1980s after an acrimonious dispute. But the past was set aside when they showed that they had the right investment approach for a return. And the Qataris were probably pleased to see that they were not wholly dependent on the giant ExxonMobil investments. Shell, along with Total, gave political as well as industrial balance to the sector. A valuable spin-off from this investment in gas has been a huge increase in oil production. The investment climate has encouraged companies to come in and reverse Qatar's declining production of 'black' oil. Together with the condensates from gas extraction, oil is now headed towards one million barrels a day, double the predicted peak just a decade ago.

HUMAN DEVELOPMENT IN THE ARAB WORLD

The income from oil and gas has made Qatar very rich; soon it will have the highest per capita income in the world. But the money means nothing if it is not spent wisely. The World Human Development Report for 2005 already has Qatar ranked first in the Arab world, and it is rapidly moving up the global ranking. Qatar is placing huge emphasis on the development of education, as well as culture and sport. The whole school system is being overhauled and a modern curriculum introduced. Education City is host to a growing number of faculties of foreign universities, offering teaching and standards which are internationally benchmarked. Sceptics, looking at the small size of Qatar's population, doubted if this would work. But they underestimated the extent of Qatar's commitment to this cause. In time, there is no reason why Qatar should not become a regional centre of excellence for education. This programme takes place through the Qatar Foundation, chaired by the Amir's Consort, Sheikha Mozah. She is no figurehead, but the driving force behind this enterprise, which has turned her into an international role model for Arab and Muslim women. The Qatar Foundation also supports a Science Park, which is aiming to make Qatar a regional centre for serious research. In addition, Qatar is hosting world class sporting events, the largest of which will be the Asian Games in 2006. The goal here is not just to gain more international recognition, but also to continue to open windows onto the wider world for this traditional society and to offer more outlets for the energies of the young population. With Qatar also building a series of world-class museums, due to open in the coming few years, Qatar is shaping a regional identity quite separate from the models elsewhere in the Gulf, including Dubai, which up to now has set the pace in regional entrepreneurship and innovative projects.

A MODEL FOR A PROGRESSIVE ISLAMIC STATE

In all this explosion of activity, Britain's role has been modest. Many British individuals have been heavily engaged in the process of transition. British institutions have lagged behind. Universities in particular could have been the main players in Education City but failed to grasp the opportunities on offer. British companies have fared better, but most see Qatar only as a market, and not as an investment opportunity, perhaps unable to grasp that such a small country can have such vast potential. Too few in Britain, including in Government, have tried to understand the unique character Qatar is developing. British policy in the nineteenth and twentieth centuries ensured that Qatar emerged as an independent state. Britain still has the chance to be a principal partner of Qatar, based not on any historic relationship, but rather on a shared vision of how a successful Qatar will establish a model for a progressive Islamic state that defies all predictions of the inevitability of conflict between Islam and the West.

BRITAIN AND THE UNITED ARAB EMIRATES

Patrick Nixon

EARLY DAYS

In surveying the history of Britain's relationship with the Trucial States which now make up the seven emirates of the United Arab Emirates I am struck that from tentative beginnings the British East India Company (EIC) was motivated by commercial and strategic interests. This at least has remained a constant in British policy until the present day.

In the seventeenth century British traders working with the EIC looked to southern Persia as an outlet for goods which the fledgling market in India could not absorb. In 1617, English traders were granted an exclusive concession at Jashk, thereby excluding competitors from Spain and Portugal. A century later in 1720 the Qasimi ruler of Ras al Khaimah forcibly established an entrepot at Basidu on the island of Qishm, thereby threatening the monopoly of revenue shared by the Persian government and the EIC. In 1727, a naval expedition of EIC ships seized from Basidu what the Company believed to be revenue due to them. So began a long period of unstable competition in the Gulf in which Ras al Khaimah's fleet fought against their Oman rivals for supremacy in the Gulf and even captured British ships. The Bombay government chose to protect the commercial interests of their trading ships by signing an agreement for commercial and political cooperation with the Sultan of Muscat and Oman in 1798. During the next two decades attacks by Qasimi vessels on British shipping prompted intervention by British naval bombardment and invasion of Ras al Khaimah in 1809 and subsequently of other

Qasimi ports. The destruction of the Ral Al Khaimah fleet in 1819 signalled the start of a more peaceful era – on the sea if not inland – based on a series of treaties of friendship and protection between the Bombay government and the tribal leaders of the coastal areas of the lower Gulf, culminating in a Perpetual Treaty of Peace in 1853.

'LOYAL FEUDATORIES'

The Government of India's growing influence in the lower Gulf was exercised through the Political Resident in Bushire to whom a Native Agent based in Sharjah reported from the 1820s. Occasional visits by the Resident and British naval vessels were sufficient to ensure that the Rulers complied with British requirements for the maintenance of stability. The next milestone which indelibly marked out the unique characteristic of the Indian Government's role in the lower Gulf was the agreement by the Rulers of the Trucial States in 1892 not to have dealings with any power other than the British government. This was followed in 1922 by further undertakings by the Rulers not to grant oil concessions to any company which was not supported by the British government. In this way the British succeeded in obtaining at virtually no cost their strategic and commercial objectives of keeping out their military and trading rivals in Europe while avoiding the burdens of colonial responsibility: the Rulers of the Gulf were what Lord Curzon described as 'loyal feudatories.'

OIL AND ECONOMIC DEVELOPMENT

Although oil concessions were negotiated with the Rulers of the Trucial States during the 1930s it was not until after the Second World War that prospecting for oil began in earnest. The British government were then obliged to take a closer interest in the internal affairs of the Trucial States. Oil company survey parties in the hinterland needed security as well as precision on desert boundaries which had never been defined. So in the twilight days of the Empire the oil companies persuaded the British government to increase their commitment and to abandon the policy of not intervening in the internal affairs of the Shaikhdoms. A British

Political Officer was posted for the first time on a permanent basis to Sharjah in 1949. In 1954 the Political Agency moved to Dubai. A Political Officer was appointed to Abu Dhabi in 1957. Only in 1961, a year after the announcement that oil had been discovered in commercial quantities, was a separate Political Agency established in Abu Dhabi.

In order to provide internal security for the oil companies the British government set up in 1951 a small force under British officers initially called the Trucial Oman Levies. They were used in 1955 to evict a Saudi force occupying one of the villages in the Buraimi oasis after the British government unilaterally withdrew from a fruitless attempt over four years to settle through arbitration the long running dispute over the allegiance of the villagers. This bold action damaged British relations with Saudi Arabia and was unwelcome to the United States. It showed how seriously the British government now took their responsibilities to intervene directly to support the rulers under their protection. Many years later when I first met the President of the United Arab Emirates, Shaikh Zayed Al Nahyan told me how deeply grateful he was to Britain for this action which he regarded as having been fundamental to the security of the Trucial States.

Gradually Britain also began to assume responsibility for the economic development of the Trucial States, though expenditure was never more than modest before the start of oil exports enabled Abu Dhabi to finance an ambitious programme throughout the Emirates. When Archie Lamb became Political Agent at Abu Dhabi in 1965 Sir Paul Gore-Booth, Permanent Under Secretary at the Foreign Office and father of David, commented on Archie's first impressions despatch that 'HM Government... see themselves pledged to a somewhat more rapid advancement in the Gulf than has taken place hitherto and, quite apart from their own wishes, the time is moving very fast and our own position may well depend on our ability to promote and guide that advance.'

BRITISH WITHDRAWAL FROM THE GULF
Implementation of the policy described by Paul Gore-Booth was interrupted by the abrupt announcement by the British

government in January 1968 of their intention to withdraw British forces completely from the Gulf by the end of 1971, leaving the seven Emirates, Qatar and Bahrain little time to prepare for independence and to manage their own defence and foreign relations. At the time of Independence in December 1971 few would have put money on the survival of the fledging federation of the United Arab Emirates. Apart from unresolved territorial disputes with Saudi Arabia and Iran, the Rulers were still being subjected to a destabilising barrage of propaganda put out by Arab nationalist regimes and encouraged by the Soviet Union. The remarkable stability, development and prosperity of the Federation today has been achieved despite the traumas of the Iranian revolution in 1979, the Iran-Iraq war in the 1980s, the invasion of Kuwait in 1990 and of Iraq in 2003. The success of the Federation is due to the courage and vision of its main architects Shaikh Zayed, Ruler of Abu Dhabi and Shaikh Rashid al Maktoum, Ruler of Dubai.

FROM MONOPOLY TO COMPETITION

Before the first exports of oil in 1962 the economies of the Emirates were on a very small scale with few imports and almost no exports. Ships of the British India Steam Navigation Company called at Dubai regularly from 1904 and Gray Mackenzie had been shipping agents in Dubai since 1891. Only in 1946 was the first branch of a British bank opened in Dubai – the Imperial Bank of Iran, later the British Bank of the Middle East. This was the launch pad of the long and distinguished career of Easa Saleh al Gurg who has played such an important role in the evolving relationship between the Emirates and Britain for sixty years, first as a banker, then as Executive Director of the Trucial States Development Office in the 1960s and for the last fourteen years as Ambassador in London. The Trucial States Development Office played a crucial role as a channel for British advice on infrastructure development which laid a foundation for the rapid economic expansion of the 1970s as the income from oil exports from Abu Dhabi and Dubai increased.

In 1971 British companies had a clear advantage in competing for construction projects and trade with the Emirates. The Rulers, especially in Dubai, relied mainly on British advisers, particularly in the fledgling Armed Forces and the Police. There were now three British banks with branches in the country: British Bank of the Middle East, Eastern Bank and Ottoman Bank. Air traffic control, telecommunications and shipping services were provided by British companies. BP and Shell were prominent in the consortia exploiting the oil fields both onshore and offshore.

Inevitably the Federation's ambitious development programme attracted worldwide interest. British companies did not have it all their own way. Many found it difficult to compete against companies from Lebanon, Egypt and the Indian sub-continent. Banks set up by Emirate interests and branches of other foreign banks ended the British monopoly in banking. The predominance of British engineering consultants and architects was gradually challenged.

DEFENCE COOPERATION

Equally inevitable was the change in the political relationship between Britain and the UAE after 1971. Following the withdrawal of British forces the two countries signed a Treaty of Friendship and Cooperation but this did not place a binding obligation on British forces to assist the UAE in times of crisis. The British government had made clear that they would not station forces east of Suez. Nevertheless from the start of the Iran-Iraq war in 1980 there was a continuous British naval presence in the Gulf of Royal Navy warships of the Armilla patrol intended to contribute to the security of oil shipments and the safe transit of shipping through the Gulf. After Iraq's invasion of Kuwait in 1990 Royal Navy vessels in cooperation with the United States and other allied navies increased their patrols to help enforce United Nations sanctions against Iraq. The UAE has for 25 years been generous in providing shore facilities in its ports for visiting RN ships.

From 1971 the UAE began to build up its own defences while relying on the United States to be the ultimate guarantor of its security. The UAE tended to look primarily to France to supply sophisticated defence equipment and training for its Armed Forces, latterly to the United States. The relatively small involvement of British companies has been a source of disappointment to those trying to promote a revival of the intimate defence relationship of the past. Various explanations are offered for this. In the 1970s and 80s, British defence equipment suppliers were unable or unwilling to meet the needs of the UAE Armed Forces on the same competitive basis as France; some of the systems supplied by British companies failed to meet the expectations of the customer; and the Emiratis compared the cost of training provided by the British Ministry of Defence unfavourably with that offered by France. As part of a renewed effort to revive British involvement with the UAE Armed Forces after the Gulf war of 1991 the British government concluded in 1996 a Defence Cooperation Accord under which Britain gave a more open ended commitment to support the UAE in times of crisis than to any other country outside NATO. Nevertheless the relationship suffered a further setback in 1999 when the UAE chose to attach a battalion of troops to the French peacekeeping contingent in Kosovo in preference to joining the British. Since then large defence contracts have continued to elude Britain as the UAE Armed Forces, under the leadership of Shaikh Mohammed bin Zayed, now Crown Prince of Abu Dhabi, have for strategic and commercial reasons sought to rely on the United States for the bulk of their defence requirements. The contract awarded to Lockheed Martin for the supply of 80 F-16 aircraft effectively locks the United States into a long-term commitment to the defence of the UAE.

TRADE

The economy of the UAE has boomed since the oil price started to rise from a low point in 1999 and following the decision of Shaikh Mohammed bin Rashid, Crown Prince of Dubai, to diversify Dubai's economy into a dizzying variety of ever bolder development projects. British engineering and design companies were responsible for the landmark Burj al Arab and Emirates Towers projects but have won relatively few of the prestigious development contracts in the face of stiff competition. Nor were BP or Shell successful in bidding for a 28 per cent stake in the development of the Upper Zakhum oilfield. The selection of Exxon Mobil in 2005 is widely seen as another strategic move by the new rulers of the UAE to increase the stake of a major US company in the economy.

The relatively low success rate of British companies in winning high profile business in the Emirates tends to mask the extent of British involvement in the economy, particularly in Dubai and Sharjah. Britain has consistently been among the top three or four sources of imports to the UAE. By 2004 the UAE had become Britain's thirteenth largest export market and its largest in the Middle East, taking £2.7 billion of British goods, a rise of thirty per cent over 2003. This remarkable growth can be attributed to the familiarity built up between traders of both countries over the last 35 years and to the very large community of British expatriates – perhaps 100,000 in all – who have found the Emirates an attractive base for business throughout the region.

PERSONAL LINKS

In common with people from other Gulf states Emiratis are probably more familiar with Britain than any other country. For thity years it has been like a second home to them. A high proportion of the first generation to be sent abroad for their tertiary education was educated in Britain. Among the political elite and the ruling families personal links were forged with Britain for a generation after the British withdrawal in 1971. British politicians and members of the British Royal Family were frequent visitors to the Emirates and some enduring friendships were formed, though never reaching the level of intimacy achieved at the highest levels in personal relationships between Britain and Bahrain or Oman.

In recent years these personal links have been in decline. Emiratis are looking further afield for holidays. Under the influence of globalised American culture, the younger generation are increasingly attracted to the United States and Australia for tertiary education, partly because entry qualifications are less demanding. As this younger generation has started to take up influential management positions over the last decade there has been a perceptible shift of focus from Britain towards the United States as the source of inspiration and partner of choice.

In intergovernmental relationships as well Britain's historical influence has been challenged, above all by the United States, which has buttressed its strategic role in defence of the UAE through close personal relationships between politicians from both Democratic and Republican administrations and key members of the ruling families of Abu Dhabi and Dubai. Other trading partners, particularly France and Germany, have developed a high level dialogue in support of efforts to win more business. In this respect British politicians are perceived by Emiratis to have been comparatively less attentive. For their part British businessmen have a tendency to attribute their lack of success in winning high profile contracts to inadequate political support. During my time in the Emirates I saw no direct evidence that British companies missed contracts which they should have won because the government did not lobby hard enough on their behalf. Indeed I sometimes had the impression that lobbying by visiting British politicians was counterproductive. There may perhaps for historical reasons have been a tendency by each to take the other for granted or conversely to expect too much. That is a legacy of a postcolonial situation, as I also found during my service in Qatar and Zambia. Below the surface however it is clear that British companies and individuals are still reaping handsomely the rewards of a special relationship developed a generation ago. Undoubtedly they will not be able to count in the future on a preference for Britain and will have to run faster to keep up with their nimble competitors.

BRITAIN AND OMAN 1650-2005

Robert Alston

The political and commercial interests of Britain and Oman have been entwined in many different contexts over the past 350 years, and particularly the last 200. Until 1947, the interests of Britain were predominantly those first of the East India Company and then of the British Government of India. The ending of Portuguese commercial domination of the Indian Ocean, the challenge of Louis XV and then Napoleon to growing British interests in India, the expansion of Wahhabism in the Arabian peninsula, the trading and political ties between Oman and East Africa, political rivalry between interior Oman on the one hand and Muscat and the Batinah Coast on the other, two world wars, the Cold War, and the importance of political stability in the Gulf as a primary conduit for world oil supplies, are just some of the issues which have impacted on them at different periods.

CHALLENGING THE PORTUGUESE

The events of the mid seventeenth century provide a kind of prologue to the story. The Portuguese had been the first, and for a century the unchallenged European power to seek control over the trade in spices and other luxury goods from the east to European markets. The ruthlessness of Captains such as Albuquerque who sacked Muscat in 1507, and the possession of gunpowder and cannon gave them control through much of the sixteenth century. The Cape route took their traffic at the expense of the previous Red Sea trade, and from the Ottoman Turks who controlled it. The first challenge to the Portuguese thus came from the Turks, who seized Muscat three times and against whom the Portuguese forts of Jalali and Mirani which dominate the Muscat skyline to this day were built in the 1580s.

The real nemesis of the Portuguese was however Shah Abbas of Iran in the first decades of the seventeenth century. His first significant dealings with Europeans were with British merchants, first arriving overland via Russia, and then from 1600 in the ships of the newly founded East India Company. British ships joined in Shah Abbas's expulsion of the Portuguese from Hormuz, their principal stronghold on the Iranian coast, in 1622. Under the leadership of Imam Nasir Ibn Murshid, the first Ya'ruba Imam of Oman, the Portuguese position there was gradually eroded and Muscat itself fell in 1649. In this context Imam Nasir sought alternative trading partners and took the initiative to offer the East India Company trading privileges in Oman. In 1646 Philip Wylde signed the first Anglo Omani Treaty providing for a trading monopoly at Sohar. A further Treaty negotiated in 1670 would have given the Company control of one of the Muscat Forts. It never came into effect but for the next century East India Company ships traded regularly with Muscat.

Over this time Oman passed through a period of unity, prosperity, and maritime strength under the Ya'rubas till 1718, then a period of civil war, and then a revival at sea and on land under Ahmad bin Said, the first ruler of the Al Bu Saidi dynasty which has continued to the present day. In this period Oman controlled both sides of the entrance to the Gulf and over half of all Gulf trade was channelled through Muscat, much of it carried in Omani ships but much in those of France and Britain. Muscat thus became one stage on which the growing rivalry between the two countries for control of the trade and influence in India itself, first in the Seven Years War and then under Napoleon, was played out.

RESISTING NAPOLEON

Napoleon's arrival in Egypt in 1799 was correctly identified in Britain as an alarming threat to Indian interests. It had been anticipated in 1798 by a mission to Sayyid Sultan, the second effective Al Bu Saidi ruler, who agreed to exclude the French (and Dutch) and to take the British part in international matters. The Wellesley brothers in India were fearful that he would be unable to resist Napoleon's blandishments to reverse this and sent Captain (later Sir John) Malcolm first to Muscat and then to Fath Ali Shah in Iran to secure British interests. The 1800 Treaty which resulted contained the often quoted phrase about the friendship of the two countries enduring 'till the end of time or the sun and moon cease in their revolving careers'. Hyperbole of course but a pointer to an ever-closer involvement of the two nations with each other over the next two centuries. The 1800 Agreement was not a one-sided one. The British recognised that they were dealing with the predominant power in the area and both sides also saw value in working together to contain the maritime threat to both from the Qawasim Sheikhs of Ras al Khaimah who were increasingly threatening the shipping of both. It also provided for the first time that 'an English gentleman of respectability shall always reside in the port of Muscat'.

Napoleon, advised by Talleyrand, did not give up. In 1803 he sent Cavaignac as Consul to Muscat, but Sayyid Sultan refused to receive him. In 1807, Sayyid Said bin Sultan, who became ruler in 1804, concluded a Treaty of Amity and Commerce with the French, but changed his mind when the French were driven out of Mauritius. Omani policy at this time was strongly influenced by the desire for British help in their ongoing conflicts both with the Qawasim and with the land based threat from the Wahhabis from the Nejd who took the Buraimi oasis in 1800 and allied themselves with the Qawasim. Sultan and then Said were in conflict with them on land and sea for the best part of two decades. In 1806 the Council in Bombay, in a breach with longstanding policy of not getting directly engaged in intra-Arab quarrels, authorised East India Company ships to get directly involved with Qawasim ships in action with the Omani fleet, albeit under strict rules of engagement. By 1821, British troops were also directly engaging Wahhabi tribes on land in eastern Oman and suffering significant casualties in the process.

SUPPORTING OMAN'S TRADING INTERESTS
The long reign of Sayyid Said from 1804 to 1856 was marked by active relationships with Britain, not only in the Indian Ocean but

in London. Once the Qawasim and Wahhabi threats had been managed with British support, Said turned to a proactive maritime policy in support of Oman's trading interests in the Gulf, Iran, and East Africa. An indefatigable traveller and trader himself, he possessed a formidable fleet, much of it constructed in the shipyards of British India. In his middle years, reflecting this prosperity and breadth of interest he exchanged gifts with William IV and Queen Victoria and sent his Ambassador on his own ship twice to London in 1837 and 1842. He presented William IV with a handsome Bombay-built ship, the *Liverpool*, which served for many years as a ship of the line in the Royal Navy.

In the second half of his life Said's interests, and indeed his residence, were increasingly focussed not on Oman but on Zanzibar. Omanis had been in East Africa since the seventh century, and Omani rulers had been in possession of Zanzibar since helping to drive out the Portuguese in the mid seventeenth century. Said was responsible for the explosion of prosperity in Zanzibar in the nineteenth century on the basis of the introduction of cloves to a climate where they thrived and which was much closer to the European markets than the East Indies from whence they originated. But it was the other main plank of East African trade which imposed considerable stress on the British-Omani relationship, and on an issue where British policy was driven not from Bombay but from London.

SUPPRESSING SLAVERY

Following the abolition of the Atlantic slave trade in 1802 the attention of the powerful abolitionist lobby in London focussed increasingly on the Indian Ocean slave trade. Of long standing, both the trade itself and the lives of the slaves once they arrived in the Arabian Peninsula avoided the worst of the horrors of the Atlantic trade and the Caribbean plantations. Nonetheless, the suppression of slavery everywhere had become an irrevocable and talismanic aim for much of British opinion which governments could not ignore even when it brought them into conflict with the interest of rulers with whom they had many other political and economic interests in common. Between 1822 and 1875 Said and his successor had no option but to accept a series of Treaties which, in return for other benefits, gradually but remorselessly eliminated the trade, with severe economic effects for Oman which contrasted sharply with the burgeoning prosperity of Zanzibar over the same period.

Sayyid Said's preoccupation with Zanzibar had significant consequences on his death in 1854. One son, Majid, assumed control of all Said's African dominions but agreed to pay an annual sum to his brother Thuwaini who had claimed the succession in Oman. Disputes arose over these sums and Thuwaini had despatched a fleet to Zanzibar to back up his claims when the British government intervened to prevent civil war. Both sided were persuaded to submit their claims to arbitration by Lord Canning, the first Viceroy of India. What was known as the Canning Award of 1862 confirmed each brother territorially but obliged Majid to pay 40,000 crowns annually to Muscat in return for Thuwaini relinquishing his claims to Zanzibar and for thee balancing of the financial assets of what were now recognised and described as two separate sovereign Sultanates, though Zanzibar was a British Protectorate where the Union Jack flew, which has never been the case in Oman.

The Omani nation as we know it today is an amalgam of two distinct social and cultural traditions reflected in the very name of the country till 1970 – Muscat and Oman. The term Muscat refers not just to the port city of that name but to the series of communities on the Gulf of Oman Coast from Sohar to Sur, half a dozen ports, Sohar, Muttrah, Muscat itself, Qalhat, Quriyat, and Sur, and a hinterland which produced the commodities they consumed and exported. These were communities which had looked out across the oceans for many centuries – Omani merchants sailed as far as China in the seventh century. Oman refers to the tribal areas mainly but not exclusively on the landward side of the Al Hajjar mountain range which lies behind the coastal plain, unchanging over many centuries and eking a living from areas of cultivable land on the rivers running off from the mountains and in some places from irrigation carried over many miles by underground canals like those in Iran.

The call of Islam reached Oman in the lifetime of the Prophet but the events which most strongly defined Omani religious culture took place among Omani tribesmen in Basra in the early years of the Ummayad caliphate. The Ibadhi tradition is very early, a century earlier than the four traditional schools of orthodox Islam. Its aim, following the splits between Ali and Mu'awiya was to restore the Islamic state to what it had been in the Prophet's lifetime. Its qualities have been described as 'Puritanism without intolerance.' Of importance throughout Omani history has been the concept that the most worthy man in the society should be chosen to exercise political as well as spiritual leadership. Though the record is incomplete Imams, including the first two Al Bu Saidi rulers, were selected to rule in Oman in this way to the end of the eighteenth century.

The concerns of British officials, whether in Bombay or London, in respect of Oman had to do above all with trade and shipping between the Gulf and India and in the Indian Ocean more widely. An independent and sturdy Muscat was an important bulwark against insecurity and piracy. They protected merchants of Indian origin, Shi'a and Hindu, in Muscat. Support for the Muscat based Al Bu Saidi dynasty against instability arising both from family feuding and from the interior tribes became a guiding thread in Britain's policies towards Oman for a century and more after the death of Sayyid Said in 1854. The British Government also assumed responsibility for the payment of the Canning Award subsidy, virtually the only source of revenue in unstable and economically lean times. In 1877 and 1883 British ships were used in support of Sultan Turki against attacks from the exterior.

RESISTING THE FRENCH, 1890 – 1905
The 1890s saw a revival of French efforts to supplant British influence and secure assets for themselves, notably in the form of a coaling station near Muscat. They also allowed slave traders to operate under the French flag, and actively supported the supply of arms across the Gulf of Oman to Baluchistan and the North West Frontier. Sultan Faisal was tempted by French blandishments to try to reduce his dependence on British support. For the first time

a French Consul M Ottavi was accepted in Muscat and, to the fury of the recently appointed Viceroy Lord Curzon, succeeded in securing a coaling concession, but this was withdrawn after stern British intervention. Probably the grandest event in the whole story of British relationships with Oman was the visit of the Viceroy in 1903, supported by seven British warships for two days of pomp and protocol culminating in a durbar on the deck of *HMS Argonaut.*

In 1915, when the two main tribal confederations came together to revive the Imamate and attack Sultan Faisal in Muscat, one of the most decisive British interventions in Omani affairs came in response to an appeal from the Sultan when a battalion of Baluch troops under British command was sent to Muscat and was crucial in the defeat of the tribal confederation at the battle of Bait Al Falaj, just outside Muscat. By this time the First World War was well under way. Britain was engaged in a campaign with Ottoman Turkish forces in Mesopotamia and the then Viceroy Lord Hardinge paid a visit to Muscat as part of a tour which had also taken him to Basrah and Kuwait.

When the war was over negotiations began to try to establish an understanding between Sultan Teimur and the interior tribes which would avert further direct attacks on Muscat. The negotiations were animated by Orde Wingate, then the British Political Agent and, after a year, resulted in the Peace of Seeb between Sultan Teimur and the Imam by which the Sultan accepted that his authority did not run in the interior in return for an agreement by the Imam not to challenge his authority elsewhere and to desist from further attack. British troops were withdrawn, but at the same time British help in the creation of an Omani standing army as well as the improvement of financial administration were stepped up. Bertram Thomas became the effective head of the Sultan's administration with, for some years, the title of Wazir, before his interest in exploration and archaeology came to take priority.

Sultan Said became Ruler in 1932 when his father abdicated, and the period between then and 1970 when he was replaced by his son, the present Ruler Sultan Qaboos, became one of increasingly direct British involvement in support of the Sultan. Both before and after 1947 the importance of Oman to Britain lay in its location. Oman lay on the route of the Imperial Airways flying boats which established the first air service between Britain and British India between the wars. During the Second World War, a number of Omani bays and landing strips became ever more significant in maintaining the link between the Middle East Theatre of war and India, especially after the beginning of the war with Japan. After 1947, and particularly in the 1950s and 1960s the Omani route was still crucial for Britain in communications with its remaining strategic interests in Malaysia and Hong Kong.

In this period, before the discovery of oil in Oman, the nation's sources of revenue were slender, whilst Sultan Said was determined that Oman should live within these slender means. He practised frugal and minimalist government and established a modus vivendi with Muhammad al Khalili who held the revived position of Imam from 1920 to 1954. However political change in the region after 1947 and the prospect of the discovery of oil in interior Oman led to the development of three externally backed challenges from 1950 in the resolution of which more direct British military support was necessary.

THE BURAIMI OCCUPATION

The Wahhabis had been turned out of the Buraimi oasis in 1870 and ceased to be a political factor in Omani history until 1950 when a force of Saudis occupied part of the oasis. Sultan Said determined to throw them out and mustered a force at Sohar to which many of the Omani tribes rallied with the support of the Imam. However the British Government, mindful of the broader scene in the Arabian Peninsula and with American backing, argued strongly that the situation should be resolved by arbitration rather than force and, with great reluctance, Sultan Said concurred. By 1955, with the arbitration process dragging on with little prospect of an acceptable outcome, British policy changed and a combined force from Oman and the Trucial Oman Scouts based in Sharjah ejected the remaining Saudis.

By 1955 a situation was developing in which for the last time there was a threat to the stability of Oman from the Imamate. Imam Muhammad al Khalili died in 1954 and was replaced, against the wishes of some important tribes, by Ghalib Ibn Ali who dreamed of the Imamate as a separate oil producing state with Saudi and Egyptian support. Sultan Said responded to this challenge by occupying the interior in December 1955, soon after the reoccupation of all of Buraimi. The sequel to this was the first ever motorised journey the length of Oman by the Sultan from Dhofar in the South, where he generally lived, through the interior to Muscat, a journey chronicled by Jan Morris.

JEBEL AKHDAR AND DHOFAR

This was the end of the Imamate but not however the end of the story. Ghalib and his brother Talib, with external support, infiltrated back into the country in May 1957 and sought to re-establish the Imamate. Sultan Said appealed for British military support which was given in the form of the Trucial Oman scouts, and a battalion of the Cameronians with RAF support. The rebels fell back into the fastnesses of the Jebel Akhdar from which they could not be dislodged. Not wanting, in the aftermath of Suez, to be sucked into a protracted guerrilla war, the British forces were withdrawn. However, in 1958, after discussions between Sultan Said and Julian Amery and then Foreign Secretary Selwyn Lloyd, it was agreed to step up British assistance to the Omani armed forces, including the creation of an Air Force and in January 1959 two Squadrons of the SAS, amongst them as a young officer Peter de la Billiere who was to lead British forces in the Gulf War of 1990, stormed the last rebel positions in the Jebel Akhdar and the threat was at an end.

There was to be one further externally backed threat to the integrity of the Omani nation, this time in the Southern region of Dhofar, adjacent to the border with Yemen.

Separated from interior Oman by hundreds of miles of baking, waterless gravel plain, Dhofar is culturally and ethnically distinct from the rest of the country but its history has been interwoven with that of Oman over the centuries. Its own golden age was as one of the great centres of the frankincense trade over 2,000 years ago. Until 1970 its links were by sea with Muscat not overland to interior Oman, and it was the preferred residence of Sultan Said through much of his life.

During the 1960s a combination of disaffected Dhofari tribesman and more educated rebels drawing on the rhetoric and ideas of both Marxism and Arab nationalism, supported from various Arab countries, developed into open revolt. They received a big boost from the British withdrawal from Aden in 1967 and by 1969 they controlled the Yemeni border and the line of hills which parallels the Coast behind Salalah, despite Sultan Said's access to British advice and equipment. It was only after Sultan Qaboos seized power from his father in June 1970 that the tide turned. Qaboos emphasised nation building, and development and issued a swift amnesty for guerrillas who were willing to abandon their revolt and join this process. Final elimination of the rebels did not come until 1975 and involved extensive British advice and equipment as well as the deployment of the SAS to apply the 'hearts and minds' techniques they had evolved during the Malayan Emergency. Often overlooked is the important contribution also made by a substantial Iranian force deployed on the instructions of the Shah in 1974 in the closing stages of the operation.

Throughout the 1960s Britain was effectively responsible for Oman's foreign affairs, and also had regularly to defend Sultan Said and his policies against UN pressure mobilised by other Arab nations.

Sultan Qaboos enjoyed advantages which had been denied to his father. The Imamate was no more and he was able to decree that the name 'Muscat and Oman' emphasising the earlier division, should be replaced by 'Sultanate of Oman'. Above all oil revenues had started to flow in 1967, modest by comparison with other regional producers, but giving him a freedom of action to implement development plans to address the needs of the Omani people on a scale which had simply not been available to his father. As the Dhofar rebellion was brought under control Oman's Renaissance could begin.

RISING PROSPERITY

After 1970 Oman's relationship with Britain became much less exclusive. Oman had never had protected status and British officials had never held formal administrative or judicial authority but there were nonetheless many reasons why Britons and British organisations and companies were involved from the outset in many aspects of this explosive change. Shell had bought out their other Iraq Petroleum Company partners and were the major force behind the development of the Omani oil and gas industry. British officers on contract had played a key role in the development of Oman's armed forces during Sultan Said's life and several of them – Malcolm Dennison and Colin Maxwell perhaps most notably – made this their life's work. After 1970, as Oman's Armed Forces grew rapidly the number of contract personnel rose at one time to over 1,000. At the same time a smaller number of Loan Service Officers – serving British officers on secondment – filled key posts initially in the command structure where many made a very significant contribution to the conclusion of the Dhofar war, and more recently in staff and training roles. By around 1990 Omani officers had been trained with the skills and experience to take the top command positions and General Johnny Watts, who had led the assault on the Jebel Akhdar in 1959 handed over the post of Commander of the Sultan's Armed Forces to an Omani officer in 1989.

The stability of the Gulf and of the oil supplies which emerge from it remained a major preoccupation of the British and other Western Governments in the 1980s and 1990s, following the Iranian Revolution and Saddam Hussein's attack on Iran in 1981.Oman's strategic position controlling the southern shore of the Strait of Hormuz, the exit from the Gulf, was and is highly significant. Sultan Qaboos pursued a strategy of diversifying diplomatic relations and joining international organisations, of emphasising particularly the building of relations with the other Gulf nations in the Gulf Cooperation Council and defining Oman's boundaries with Saudi Arabia for the first time, of maintaining a dialogue with the Revolutionary Government in Iran, and of building up Oman's armed forces to make her once again a significant regional power. This made him over those years an important interlocutor for successive British governments. Margaret Thatcher in particular regarded him as one of Britain's most significant partners on regional issues. Britain's two biggest post war exercises to test tri-service ability to deploy significant forces outside the NATO area – Saif Sareea I and II – both took place in Oman, in 1986 and 1999, and the lessons of the latter proved a huge benefit when such a deployment was needed at the end of 1990 to help to reverse Saddam Hussein's invasion of Kuwait, as did the Sultan's willingness to provide staging facilities and other support for the build-up.

British businesses have played an active part in the revival of the Omani economy in the past forty years. I have already mentioned Shell. A few other companies were active before 1970. The British Bank of the Middle East (now part of HSBC) had been present for many years and Peter Mason, its long serving Manager in Muscat, was a trusted personal adviser both to Sultan Said and Sultan Qaboos. Trading companies like Grey Mackenzie have had relationships going back many years. But there was a rapid growth after 1970. Much of it related to the servicing of the needs of the growing oil and gas industry and the building of the basic infrastructure of a nation which is, after Saudi Arabia, the largest in the GCC. Many of Britain's major contractors, such as Taylor Woodrow, Wimpey, and Costain, entered into joint ventures with Omani partners. Technical support for the equipment of the growing Sultan's Armed Forces brought in companies like British Aerospace and Airwork. In 1989 the Omani British Friendship Society, made up of senior business leaders from both countries, was set up to act as a bilateral business council and a focus for the development of trade in both directions.

RELATIONS SINCE 1985

By the mid-1980s the British community in Oman was over ten thousand strong and it has fluctuated around a figure a little lower than that for most of the time since. In addition to the armed forces, the oil industry, and the business community, Britons have involved themselves in a whole host of other areas of growth and development, teaching at all levels, medical services, the environment and the arts. One of the most remarkable were the dedicated team who arrived, on Sultan Qaboos's instruction in 1985 with orders to create, from a situation where no Omani other than a few military bandsman had any experience of western music, the Oman Symphony Orchestra which is now an experienced and professional ensemble.

In 1989 the relationship in all its dimensions was celebrated in a diverse programme of events in Oman called 'Oman with Britain', a name personally endorsed by Sultan Qaboos. In summing up the relationships I have outlined in this chapter and the relationship as it exists today I can do no better that repeat what I said in the Introduction which I had the pleasure to contribute to the brochure supporting the exhibition put together by Michael Rice and called 'Oman with Britain – Bilateral Relations from the Seventeenth Century to the Present Day.'

Maritime trading interests first brought the two peoples together: nautical and merchantile traditions are deeply engrained in each nation's history. While trading interest provided the initial contact, the relationship between the two countries was soon expanded to the basis of shared interests in the Indian Ocean. This long relationship based on mutual interests grew naturally into one of mutual respect, trust and friendship. That friendship has been twice tested in conflicts in which British and Omani servicemen have fought – and died- in the cause of the stability and prosperity of modern Oman.

I added the hope that Oman with Britain would 'be a contribution to ensuring that the relationship has a healthy future as well as a long past. Friendship between individuals is no different from friendship between states; it should be kept in constant repair'.

THE MIDDLE EAST IN LONDON

Paul Tempest

The Middle East in London' was a major exhibition and conference with Seminars held in June 2001 at the School for Oriental and African Studies in London under the patronage of HRH The Prince of Wales. Numerous papers had been commissioned from academics, business and finance leaders, media specialists, historians, artists and diplomats. The aim was to distil from these inputs an essence and an overview of the Middle East presence in London covering Business and Finance, Art, Collections and Collectors, History, Media, Culture, Social Issues, Cinema and Performance Arts and Politics. Under the direction of Sarah Stewart of SOAS and the skilful editorship of Caroline Singer, the conclusions were carefully woven together to provide a richly-illustrated volume The Middle East in London (Stacey International, London, 2002). The opening keynote address was by Dr Hanan Ashrawi and former Foreign Secretary, the Rt Hon. Lord Howe of Aberavon provided a long and masterly drawing-together of the various threads in his Concluding Remarks.

Lord Howe began his Concluding Remarks by pointing out that the conference provided overwhelming evidence that London still plays a pivotal role in the Middle East region – as a centre of financial and political activity, for the gathering of intelligence and the dissemination of news and influence. As Charles Richards had pointed out 'London is much closer to the Middle East than Washington' and speaker after speaker emphasised that clear-minded observers in the Arab world know that London remains just as important in the area as ever. This is not to say that, even if London still holds the number one position, it can remain complacent – there are now many new capitals wishing to compete with London.

AN IMMENSE DIVERSITY – THE TERRORISM ISSUE

Lord Howe continues:

An important feature about the Arab presence is its immense diversity. It is not just a diversity between the different nations whose peoples have come here in such numbers. Often the conflicts within each of the national groups represented here are much more serious than any wider differences. This is because so many people have over the years relied upon our asylum laws to offer them some refuge from persecution at home. And, as I was often reminded during my days at the Foreign Office, Arab governments "frequently express their anger and dismay" at our tolerance.

One consequence of this relationship, ironically enough, has been the extent to which Britain (and Britons) have sometimes been targeted by Middle-Eastern terrorists – and thus almost instinctively aligned in anti-terroristm partnership with the United States. Alongside our long-standing Special Relationship, this might be one explanation of the phenomenon described by Sir James Craig, whereby British governments tend to follow the Americans at the same time as we have, in his words, "been trying to persuade the Americans to be more even-handed on Middle-Eastern issues".

Lord Howe goes on to argue that terrorism can never lay the foundation for lasting peace, but neither can that be laid by those who strive to crush terror by force alone – without regard for the root causes of terror. How right he was – as the responses to September 11, 2001, Afghanistan, in Iraq and in the recent London bombings have demonstrated.

A LARGE AND GROWING ARAB COMMUNITY
The Arab community in London and the rest of the United Kingdom, supported by its own leading Arabic newspapers, magazines and media networks, is large and active, but only rarely visible. It is deeply embedded in British public life and, as a part of the much larger Islamic community in the UK, it plays a dynamic and valuable part in our national life.

LONDON AS A FINANCIAL CENTRE

Since 1973-4 much of the vast new surpluses of the OPEC countries and other Arab oil-producing states began to flow through London giving new stimulus to the real estate, foreign exchange and other financial markets. Deregulation and privatisation in the UK energy and other industries gave new opportunities for Middle East investors and the London capital market was well-equipped to channel these funds into productive investment worldwide. These well-used investment paths through London have already turned into stable and reliable highroads in the global financial network and regulatory system. Today one third of the total world turnover in foreign exchange is conducted through London and financial services in the UK represent six per cent of UK Gross National Product and employ over a million people.

A 2,000 YEAR OLD LINKAGE

As Professor Fred Halliday put it, London was founded 2,000 years ago by an empire which at the same time ruled Carthage, Alexandria, Jerusalem, Damascus and Constantinople. The oldest place of worship in London – in Queen Victoria Street in the heart of the City – is the Temple of Mithras, a Zoroastrian god popular with Asian soldiers serving with the Roman legions. The most important square in London carries an Arabic name – taraf al-gharra, Trafalgar or 'the way of beauty'.

PROSPECTS AND OPPORTUNITIES

Paul Tempest

K uwait, Bahrain, Qatar, UAE and Oman are a source of astonishment to all – including the contributors to this volume – who first knew the Gulf well over forty years ago and who, since then, have witnessed at close quarters, what has been an almost totally peaceful transition to robust, affluent and dynamic modern economies.

It is true that the eight Gulf states are blessed with bounteous natural resources and that Iran, Iraq and Saudi Arabia dominate in terms of population, land area and the past production of hydrocarbons. Yet each of the governments of the five other Gulf states deserve credit for adapting flexibly to changing circumstances, seizing their opportunities for development, avoiding external and internal threat and confrontation and nonetheless preserving the basic character of their traditional life.

For all the Gulf governments today, however, there is little room for complacency. The five states covered in this volume have to look no further than the Iraqi invasion and occupation of Kuwait in 1990-91 to be aware of their fragility in terms of defending their own territory against more numerous and well-equipped neighbours and against the incursions of terrorists and infiltrators intent on destabilising the fabric of their traditional societies. These governments are fully aware of long-standing claims to their territory and also have to take account of the very mixed character of their populations. As they open up their economies to globalised markets, to increasing access by the world's press and media, and to very many new residents, visitors and tourists, it is not surprising that they proceed with forethought, backed by careful step-by-step implementation and a discreet caution.

Today, the Gulf States are faced with three new challenges:

Vast new spending power provided by steeply rising oil prices – here there are challenges for accelerated development and overseas investment, but also the risks of inflation and economic overheating.

A population explosion which stretches employment opportunities to the limit – here there are risks of rising unemployment and underemployment levels and of the strains of distinguishing between legitimate employment expectations of Gulf nationals and the need to admit many more expatriates.

A shift in political orientation from West to East. Fifteen years ago two thirds of Gulf oil and gas exports were still flowing to Europe and the Americas. Today, two-thirds flow East to China, Japan and South-East Asia. This shift continues as most of the new long-term gas supply contracts are with customers to the East. Already those new customers in the East are beginning to consider how to ensure the security of their new energy supplies.

A much wider issue over the next twenty – and probably over the next fifty years – is whether the Gulf producers really can, as a group, produce adequate incremental oil and gas to match expected rising global energy demand. Many are doubtful given the unsettled politics of the region, and the barriers presented by some governments and their national oil and gas companies to access by the major multinationals and those other global companies capable of stimulating up-to-date technological change in exploration, production and refining and able to mobilise adequate capital investment.

This political and commercial uncertainty has imposed a high 'Middle East premium' on world oil prices, now double where they were two to three years ago. There is little sign of relief from this uncertainty stemming from the Middle East. It is headed by current tumult in Iraq, a shift back towards fundamentalism in Iran, the lack of success in eliminating terrorist activity in Pakistan and Afghanistan, and also the lack of progress in creating the state of Palestine and in resolving the Arab/Israeli confrontation on the West Bank and within Israel.

SOME FUNDAMENTAL POINTS MADE IN THIS VOLUME

The British are no longer the leading foreign players in the Middle East. Their moment as leaders in the Middle East ended fifty years ago in the Suez crisis of 1956, and their formal Treaty obligations to the Gulf States regarding defence and foreign affairs finally vanished with the full independence of the Lower Gulf in 1971.

The legacy of active cooperation and accumulated trust is as positive as ever. The awareness in the Gulf that the UK has always, as a staunch friend and ally, produced military, diplomatic and other support in times of crisis, (as in Kuwait, Buraimi and Oman, for example) is alive and well.

The British expatriate population in the five Gulf States is large – and larger than it has ever been. It is still growing vigorously. There are very, very few points of friction between the British expatriates and the Gulf nationals.

The United Kingdom still plays a pivotal educational role in the five smaller Gulf States. The generations who are now in the key positions of influence were largely educated in British universities, at the RMA Sandhurst and in other British educational and vocational training institutions. The British Council has a long and distinguished record in stimulating the teaching of English and providing educational opportunities in the five states.

The City of London remains just as important to the Gulf area as ever – as a centre of financial activity and as a conduit for the investment of surplus revenue whether held by the governments or in private hands.

The five Gulf States have a firm basis for their success. Their administration and commerce are firmly based on the rule of law and sound government. They deal easily and cordially with governments and companies worldwide. Their relative affluence, secure and peaceful development and high rate of economic growth can also be traced to a strong maritime and trading history (over a period of 3,000 years), to political (and religious) tolerance, to the welcome given to outside technology and skills and to the effective development of the potential of their own nationals.

The five states provide a useful model for the rest of the Islamic world.

They refute the assumption of an inevitable conflict between Islam and the West. They demonstrate how gradual liberalisation and integration of the whole community into a modern state does not imply the destruction of traditional values or the erosion of national independence.

Britain, as a friend and close ally, must cherish and renew these ties of friendship. Friendship between states is no different from friendship between individuals – it must be on an equal footing and it must be kept alive and flourishing and in constant repair.

The five states can also derive much benefit from a partnership with Britain, a country no longer in the front line of world power politics, yet who, particularly in moments of upheaval and crisis, retains their affection and trust.

THE VIEWS OF THE INTERNATIONAL ENERGY INDUSTRY
The future, the oil and gas multinationals will tell you, is always uncertain. There will be many cross-currents, fears and surprises. Yet investment in energy resources is a matter of holding your breath for decades and, more often than not, half- and quarter-centuries. The industry has to rely on its best guess, and although it can never be sure, it frequently has to invest heavily today in assets unlikely to be yielding a return until a decade has elapsed and it has to have a plan for a production life of a further twenty, thirty or forty years. Essential in this process is the industry's view of future energy supply and demand and what impact supply and demand will have on the price of oil and other forms of energy.

The industry view of future oil prices has changed over the past two to three years. A major factor has been the buoyancy of global energy demand, now predicted by the International Energy Agency in Paris to rise by 60 per cent (the base-case scenario) by

2030 with 85 per cent of the increment supplied by fossil fuels mainly oil. Most of that incremental oil and gas would have to come from the eight producers of the Gulf who sit on 60 per cent of the proven global reserves of oil and 40 per cent of those of natural gas.

The key question is whether the Gulf producers can and will produce all that extra oil and gas. They have little revenue incentive to invest heavily in much new production capacity – a tightening market with rising prices will certainly, in any case, deliver much higher revenue from oil and gas exports – perhaps double within ten years. There are other factors: Iraq is a major uncertainty; Iran still largely isolated; China, with vast energy import dependence, is already taking over from Japan as the lead-consumer in South East Asia. Faced with political uncertainties in the Middle East, the industry and producer governments have been slow to invest adequately and there is considerable doubt that adequate capital and skills can be mobilised in time.

Others argue that rising energy prices will eventually produce new solutions to fill the supply gap – bio-fuels, much more nuclear, also solar, wind, tidal power and breakthroughs in producing heavy oil, tar sands and shales as well as improved coal production through liquefaction and gasification. The problem is that the cost and scale of most of these new technologies are at present far too high for immediate commercialisation.

What we can be fairly sure of is that the Gulf producing states will be close to the epicentre of the global economy. Their greatly enhanced revenue will trigger accelerated industrial and infrastructure investment in each of the states and there will be another surge of surplus revenue available for investment outside the Gulf.

What impacts might all this have on the United Kingdom? I propose to focus on three areas: the UK oil and natural gas industry; the UK financial services sector and the impact on the UK's ability to compete internationally.

LINKAGES BETWEEN UK AND GULF OIL AND GAS

There are already very close relationships between the oil and gas industries in the United Kingdom and the five Gulf States. The UK was prominent in the exploration and discoveries in Kuwait in the 1930s and after the Second World War seized every opportunity to explore in Qatar and UAE and later in Oman.

It is an historical irony that without the quadrupling of oil prices resulting from the oil price confrontation of 1973-74 generated first by Libya and then through the other members of OPEC including Saudi Arabia, Iran, Iraq, Kuwait, Qatar and UAE, the development of the newly discovered and high-cost oil and gas resources of the North Sea would certainly have been much more difficult and protracted.

One significant link between the UK and the Gulf is the benchmark for global oil prices. The Brent crude futures price administered by the International Petroleum Exchange in London, together with the West Texas Intermediate price used by the New York Mercantile Exchange in New York, sets the reference price by which oil transactions are agreed throughout the world.

Technology is another area which links the UK to the Arab oil and gas producers. North Sea deep-water technology in often-hostile weather and adverse climatic conditions stands firmly on the frontier of the industry's knowledge and experience. Much of the drive to innovate comes from UK and Norwegian experience in the North Sea, US experience in the Gulf of Mexico and from production off Brazil and West Africa. The Gulf producers, working in a more benign climate and environment, benefit from this in being able to select what they need from this proven new technology to achieve greater efficiency in their own operations.

Today, as the UK currently returns to high gas import dependency and, probably within five years, to steeply rising oil import dependency, there is likely to be acute pressure on the UK industry to apply the very latest technology and additional capital to prolong declining domestic production as long as possible. Our Gulf friends will be watching closely: it may well be that the long-standing flow of capital and skills from the UK to the Gulf will be reversed.

OPPORTUNITIES FOR THE UK FINANCIAL SERVICES SECTOR
From the outset of banking in the Gulf States, British banks were at the forefront in establishing branches (1920 in Bahrain, 1944 in Kuwait). The Bank of England drafted the original currency legislation and seconded staff to help set up the new currency boards, later transformed into fully-fledged central banks. Thus the new supervisory authorities were able to operate from the start within a secure legal, commercial and accountancy framework.

Despite the rapid expansion of banking activity in the Gulf, links with London remain strong and cordial. A prime example was during the Iraqi occupation of Kuwait when the Bank of England acted swiftly to freeze Iraqi funds and to help mobilise ample Kuwaiti funds for the use of the Kuwaiti Government and many Kuwaiti institutions in exile in London.

As a result of the recent steep rise in oil prices, a new wave of incremental oil revenue will be seeking investment outlets in London and elsewhere, presenting a wide range of opportunity to the UK financial service sector.

OPPORTUNITIES FOR INCREASED INTERNATIONAL TRADE
Total British exports of goods and services to Saudi Arabia, Kuwait, Bahrain, Qatar, UAE and Oman have increased by some thirty to fifty per cent in 2005. Prospects for continued growth are good. As the UK moves back over the next five years into import dependency on oil and gas, the value of an expanding export market will begin to be fully appreciated.

Over the past twenty years, the UK market share in the Gulf has fallen. Complacency and neglect have taken their toll. The Committee on Middle East Trade (COMET), highly efficient in its heyday, has been disbanded. The Middle East Association (MEA) is still a most useful London meeting-point and source of information, but it has suffered from a steady erosion of public and private sector sponsorship.

With the recent marked upturn in bilateral trading between the United Kingdom and the Gulf, it is time to change gear and seize the new opportunities that are opening in both the export goods and services sectors. With relatively little extra funding, the MEA, the British Council, the British Society of Middle East Studies (BRISMES), the Council for Anglo-Arab Understanding and other long-standing associations covering the Middle East could all play a much more vigorous part in helping to sustain such a revival of commercial activity.

AN ENDURING FRIENDSHIP

The relationship between the UK and the five Gulf states covered in this book was never a colonial relationship. The Gulf states have never lost their age-old independence and are justly proud of a maritime and trading history, which stretches over three millennia.

Over the last half-century, the British presence has become essentially commercial in character. The British expatriates thrive in the Gulf environment and the Gulf nationals feel at home in London and elsewhere in the United Kingdom. The two expatriate communities in the UK and the Gulf and the flows of visitors between the two are all larger than they have ever been and represent a dense network, on equal terms, of business partnership and friendship, an asset of lasting value to both sides.

TRIBUTES TO SIR DAVID GORE-BOOTH

KCMG, KCVO

HE KHALED AL-DUWAISAN

It is with the deepest regret I received the sad news of the passing away of David. He was one of a very rare breed, a man of world stature, a statesman of vision and a politician of immense moral conviction. David was a man of great integrity and modesty. His loss is a shock to myself and I am sure he will be terribly missed by all those who knew him. I had a remarkable working relationship with David – his help will be sorely absent in the future. He will always be remembered as an immense friend of Kuwait.

HE HRH PRINCE TURKI AL-FAISAL
(Speaking at the second WEG Memorial Lecture held in the Kuwait Embassy on 5 April 2005)

Sir David Gore-Booth was an outstanding British Ambassador to Saudi Arabia. Since his retirement from the British Foreign Service, he has worked tirelessly through HSBC, the Windsor Energy Group and many other channels to strengthen Anglo-Arab understanding. We will all miss him greatly as a wise counsel, a helpful colleague and a good friend.

HE NASSER BIN HAMAD AL-KHALIFA
(Speaking at the first WEG Memorial Lecture held in Windsor Castle on 22 January 2005)

I consider it a great privilege to have been invited to introduce and chair the first of this series of Windsor Energy Group Memorial Lectures. The relationship my country shares with the United Kingdom is perhaps best described as 'distinct' in that it has offered continued opportunity for effective cooperation. Over the last four years in London, I have been very pleased to host and participate in the Windsor Energy Group Ambassador Dinners, briefings and meetings. We will sadly miss the charm and judgement of the WEG Chairman, but we will do all we can to perpetuate the spirit of understanding and mutual respect which Sir David invariably brought to the table and to the rostrum.

HE SHEIKH KHALID BIN AHMED AL-KHALIFA
(Speaking at the third WEG Memorial Lecture held in the Bahrain Embassy on 5 April 2005)

David Gore-Booth first came to Bahrain in 1965 and since was always a most welcome visitor and guest in Bahrain. Today, we have invited Sir Roger Tomkys, former British Ambassador in Bahrain, to give the second WEG Memorial Lecture as a preliminary to the regular Quarterly Briefing of the London Diplomatic Community by the Windsor Energy Group. I am most gratified to see that there are over fifty representatives present, including several Ambassadors who have become close colleagues and also some very good friends of Bahrain. I welcome you all. These meetings and lectures will help to remind us of the inspiration and diplomacy of our much-missed WEG Chairman, Sir David Gore-Booth.

AMBASSADOR GHAYTH ARMANAZI

It was two years ago that David called me to ask for a lift to Windsor Castle to attend what has now become the WEG annual fixture. He had heard that I was driving there and returning the same evening, and he explained that it would be the most comfortable option for him given the debilitating treatment that he was receiving for his cancer. Despite his condition he insisted that he would not let WEG down and would attend at least the greater part of the weekend gathering.

To me that was typical of David; he cast his own obvious discomfort – even suffering – to one side and insisted on fulfilling the responsibilities that he had undertaken. He was also always conscious of the reliance others placed on him, and did all he could to redeem that reliance.

I did not know then, and nor, possibly, did he, that that would be the last Windsor Castle meeting which he would attend. The end when it happened, in October 2004, came as a shock, although most of us had guessed that his condition was serious, and probably getting worse. He was, of course, always the last to reveal what he was going through, and at every meeting, and work or social occasion, it was 'business as usual': David Gore Booth agonising over the 'bad news' from the Middle East but always keeping his sense of humour and never short of anecdotal gems.

What always struck me about David was his ability to reconcile a strong tendency towards advocacy with an appealing readiness to also listen, and to respect the opinion of others. Not for him was the haughty 'I know best' attitude of many with barely half his insight, intelligence and experience.

The memories he leaves behind, and the many friendships he formed, bear witness to the rare qualities of a man whose loss is deeply-felt, but also well-compensated for by the example he set.

THE MEMORIAL SERVICE ADDRESS

THE RT HON. THE LORD HOWE OF ABERAVON CH QC

Text of the Memorial Address given by Lord Howe at St Margaret's, Westminster on 16 March 2005

I dare say some of you are wondering – as I confess I did, when Mary first shared the thought with me – why an ageing, Wykehamist lawyer should have the privilege of following Julian's deeply moving tribute to his father; and also speaking today in grateful memory of a sadly so short-lived, meteoric, Etonian diplomat. But then, I recalled the 'bonding experience' – rather like being roped together on the same mountain – which David and I had shared. We had both been confronted – no other word will do – by the Scott Inquiry.

Those proceedings trampled unfairly on many – and on David, more than most. 'No civil servant', he said, in his characteristically candid Valedictory Dispatch, 'should thus be put in a position' – and this is what actually happened to him, on no mean scale – 'where he or she is pilloried in public – and mimicked on the radio, television and stage – without the chance to defend him or herself.'

Becoming thus, through no fault of his own, a media magnet surely played a part in shaping the premature conclusion of a sparkling diplomatic career.

David had, he once said, promised himself that, as the son of a diplomat of huge distinction, he would never follow the same path. Happily, however, both heredity and environment leant heavily the other way. He was conceived, remarkably it may be thought, on the *Nile* (an Egyptian merchant ship, which was taking his parents home from Tokyo, whence they had been expelled, some months after Japan's entry into the War). He was born in Washington, in 1943 – an event proclaimed in a communiqué issued by the ambassador's wife, Lady Halifax. Said David's revered mother – happily with us here today and to whom all our hearts go out – 'I don't think we've finished yet'. And – believe it or not, unlike the doctors – she was right. Almost eight hours later, David was indeed joined – or, perhaps more accurately, re-joined – by his twin brother.

Christopher recalls he was a 'smashing', 'fantastic' elder brother. Not a natural athlete but amazingly competitive – in every game from soccer to cricket to snooker, to l'Attaque – and all those other board games we used to play as children. Fearless in his tackle, keeping wicket with incredible intensity – contesting erroneous umpires' decisions with outrageous sincerity. That phrase of Christopher's captures so much, doesn't it, of the David we all knew?

From the age of fifteen, his brother observed, he was committed to hard work, knew exactly what he wanted to do with his life and pursued his goal with relentless intensity. I know much less of that, of course, than many who are here today. But for all those who worked with him – whether as colleague or as client – David was a different kind of diplomat.

For those younger than himself, in particular, he was always something of a hero. With a sense of humour and a sense of proportion, as well as a sense of fun, he was always prepared to question the conventional wisdom; and to speak up for what he believed to be right or true. It was, of course, that inability to dissemble, or to disguise his feelings, that sometimes got him into hot water.

And yet it was that very quality that made him, particularly for those outside the Office, one of those whom many admired the most – as 'a breath of fresh air in the corridors of power', 'an inspiration to those around him', 'a man of integrity whom many nowadays would do well to take as an example', and so on. The letters that came to comfort Mary and his family, after David's cruel and courageous death, are full of such praise.

'SHEER GUSTO AND VITALITY' AT THE UN

I first had the chance to work with him when he was Head of Chancery at our United Nations Mission in New York - and I was a very neophyte Secretary of State. And I have to say that I was almost bowled over by his sheer gusto and vitality. But delighted by his success in procuring access to events like Pavarotti in Tosca at the Met or Sarah Vaughan in a Harlem nightspot.

More seriously, I remember how he played a crucial part in the 1985 success of Britain's chairmanship of the 40th Anniversary meeting of the Security Council (with, most memorably, a Foreign Minister in every one of the fifteen Council seats). This high-profile event was threatened by an attempted anti-British demarche in another forum – to use the diplomatic jargon.

Our then Head of Mission, John Thomson, deputed David to head that off – by stonewalling in a lonely position, until the relevant deadline was passed. John was confident, just as soon as he said that, that the deed was as good as done. And he was absolutely right.

David's predecessor as New York Head of Chancery, Mig Goulding, had set standards, which John Thomson thought could never be matched. But David did so handsomely. He was seen as superbly qualified for that Ambassadorship, in due course. It was the job, in and from which, David had so hoped to retire from the Service – but which was, at the end, to elude him.

AN UNQUALIFIED SUCCESS IN SAUDI ARABIA

It was, of course, the Middle East to which he devoted the larger part of his life: Beirut, Baghdad, Tripoli, Jeddah and finally, Riyadh. At the age of 49, then our youngest ever British Ambassador to the Kingdom of Saudi Arabia, where he was, by anyone's standards, an unqualified success: hugely popular with the many, often demanding, British residents – and uniquely respected, loved and admired by the much wider Arab community.

David was by no means the only member of his profession to suffer from the unjust curse of being labelled a snob or a 'toff', but nothing could have been further from the truth. One of his closest friends was the miner's son (one of only three grammar school boys in his first year at Christ Church), with whom – thanks to an undisclosed ruse by his own father – David found himself sharing rooms during his three years at Oxford. Like everyone with whom David came into contact, this literally lifelong friend proclaimed his total lack of stuffiness or self-regard, his complete lack of 'side'.

He never failed to encourage the younger, less senior members of any group with whom he worked. In that spirit, one legacy that he left behind him at the Riyadh Embassy was a much-needed extension of the swimming pool. He achieved that with the help of just one exhibit: by getting the entire embassy staff to stand in the tiny old pool – it was standing room only – and there to be photographed.

'HE WAS OUR MENTOR' – NEW DELHI AND HSBC

To no-one's surprise, David's style was quite unchanged when he realised that New Delhi was destined to be his last post in the Service – and he was enthusiastically reborn, as a banker. 'He was our mentor', said his team of new colleagues at HSBC, 'he inspired us, encouraged us and enlightened us, with his humanity and understanding'.

But nothing in life was more important for David than his love for Mary. His noble management of the ending of his first marriage, with his personal thanks to Jill, and I quote his own words, 'for giving up under the strain after only a few years', was followed by the joy with which he embraced the real family life that Mary was able to give him and their children.

He was an extraordinary man – and they were extraordinarily fortunate to have found each other. He lived his all too short life to the full – and with devotion to the highest standards of the Service, which he adored. In the closing words of his famous Valedictory, 'I have hugely enjoyed a career that has always been colourful and at times controversial.' But now it is time to go home.

AUTHOR BIOGRAPHIES

SIR DAVID GORE-BOOTH KCMG KCVO (1943 – 2004) was educated at Eton College and Christ Church, Oxford. He entered the Foreign Office in 1964 and attended the Middle East Centre for Arab Studies (MECAS) , Lebanon to study Arabic in 1964 to 1966. After postings to Baghdad, Lusaka and Tripoli, he was appointed in 1978, First Secretary at the UK Permanent Representation to the European Communities in Brussels, and in 1974 Assistant Head of the Financial Relations Department in the Foreign and Commonwealth Office, London. He went on to be Counsellor in Jedda in 1980 and Counsellor and Head of Chancery in the UK Mission to the United Nations in New York in 1983. From there he went on in 1987 to be Head of the Policy Planning Staff of the FCO, and Assistant Under Secretary of State (Middle East) from 1989 to 1993. He was appointed Ambassador to Saudi Arabia in 1993 and High Commissioner, New Delhi in 1996 to 1998.

On retirement, he joined the Hong Kong and Shanghai Banking Corporation (HSBC) as special adviser to the Chairman and was soon on the board of several of the group's affiliates, travelling widely and often to very many meetings and conferences.

In London in 1999, he became the founder-Chairman of the Windsor Energy Group and he was an active member in a range of organisations, including the Middle East Association, Middle East International magazine, the Arab-British Chamber of Commerce and the Next Century Foundation. He succumbed to cancer on 31 October 2004.

SIR JAMES CRAIG GCMG graduated in Oriental languages (Arabic and Persian) at Oxford and became Lecturer in Arabic at

Durham University. In 1948 he was seconded to the Foreign Office as Principal Instructor at the Middle East Centre for Arab Studies in Shemlan, Lebanon. He joined the Foreign Office substantively in 1956, serving as HM Political Agent in the Trucial States, First secretary, Beirut, Counsellor and Head of Chancery, Jeddah, and Head of Near East and North Africa Department, Foreign and Commonwealth Office, London. He was Ambassador to Syria between 1976 and 1979, and to Saudi Arabia from 1979 to 1984.

On retirement he became Visiting Professor in Arabic at Oxford, Director-General and subsequently President of the British Society for Middle East Studies (BRISMES), Chairman of the Anglo-Arab Association, and several other committees and conferences connected with the Middle East.

In addition to many contributions to the academic journals, he is the author of *Shemlan, A History of the Middle East Centre for Arab Studies* (Macmillan, 1998).

RICHARD MUIR CMG was educated at The Stationers Company School and the University of Reading. He entered HM Diplomatic Service in 1964 and attended MECAS, Lebanon in 1965 to 1967. After postings to Jedda, Tunis and Washington, he was seconded to the Department of Energy in 1979 to 1981. He was appointed to be Director-General of the British Liaison Office, Riyadh in 1981 to 1985.

Posted back to London in 1985, he was Head of Information Department 1987 to 1990, Principal Finance Officer and Chief Inspector of the Diplomatic Service in 1991 to 1994. He was appointed Ambassador to Oman in 1994 to 1999 and to Kuwait in 1999 to 2002. After retirement, he became Chairman of the Anglo-Omani Society in 2004 and has been active in several other organisations connected with the Middle East.

SIR ROGER TOMKYS KCMG was educated at Bradford Grammar School and Balliol College, Oxford where he was a Domus Scholar. He entered HM Diplomatic Service in 1960, proceeding to MECAS (1960 to 1962), Amman (1962 to 1964) and Benghazi (1967 to 1969).

Posted back to London, he joined the Planning Staff before being appointed Head of Chancery in Athens in 1972 to 1975 followed by a secondment for two years to the Cabinet Office. In 1977 to 1980 he was Head of Near East and North Africa Department and in 1980 to 1981 Counsellor in Rome.

He was appointed Ambassador to Bahrain in 1981 to 1984, and to Syria in 1984 to 1986. After two London appointments as Assistant and then Deputy Under Secretary of State, FCO, he was appointed High Commissioner in Kenya in 1990 to 1992.

On retirement, he served as the Master of Pembroke College Cambridge from 1992 to 2004.

SIR GRAHAM BOYCE KCMG was educated at Hurstpierpoint College and Jesus College Cambridge. He joined HM Diplomatic Service in 1968, serving in Ottowa (1971), MECAS (1972 to 1974), Tripoli (1974 to 1977), Kuwait (1981 to 1985) and Stockholm (1987 to 1990). He was appointed Ambassador and Consul-General to Qatar in 1990 to 1993, to Kuwait in 1996 to 1999 and to Egypt in 1999 to 2001.

After retirement he was appointed Vice Chairman of VT International Services in 2002, and, in 2005, Joint Chairman (with Lord Howell of Guildford) of the Windsor Energy Group, London.

PATRICK NIXON CMG OBE was educated at Downside and Magdalene College, Cambridge. He joined HM Diplomatic Service in 1965 and attended MECAS, Lebanon in 1966 to 1968, serving subsequently in Cairo, Lima, Tripoli and New York. He was Head of the Near East and North African Department in FCO, London from 1983 to 1987.

He was Ambassador and Consul-General in Qatar from 1987 to 1990, High Commissioner in Zambia from 1994 to 1997, Director FCO in 1997 to 1998 and Ambassador to UAE from 1998 to 2003.

After retirement he was appointed, in 2004, Regional Coordinator for the Coalition Provisional Authority in Southern Iraq based in Basra.

ROBERT ALSTON CMG was educated at Ardingley College and New College, Oxford. After holding HM Diplomatic Service postings in Kabul, Paris and Tehran, he was appointed Head of the Joint Nuclear Unit, FCO from 1978 to 1981, Political Counsellor with the UK Delegation to NATO from 1981 to 1984, and Head of Defence Department, FCO from 1984 to 1986.

He was appointed Ambassador to Oman in 1986 to 1990, seconded to the Northern Ireland Office in 1990 to 1992 and was Assistant Under Secretary of State in the FCO in 1992 to 1994. From 1994 to 1998 he was High Commissioner to New Zealand, Governor of Pitcairn, Henderson, Ducie and Oeno Islands and High Commissioner to Western Samoa.

After retirement he has been Adviser to International Trade and Investment Missions Ltd, Trustees Representative at the Commonwealth Institute, director of the Romney Resource Centre, Consultant on Anglican Communion affairs to the Archbishop of Canterbury, Trustee of the Antarctic Heritage Trust and Deputy Lieutenant, Kent.

PAUL TEMPEST was educated at Manchester Grammar School (Foundation Scholar), on National Service in the Royal Engineers and at St Edmund Hall, Oxford (Open Scholar). He attended MECAS from 1966 to 1968. He was at the Bank of England from 1959 to 1983, including secondments to the Bank for International Settlements, as General Manager of the Qatar and Dubai Currency Board in 1970-71 and to British Gas in 1981-83. He spent two years with the World Bank in Washington (1983 to 1985) and six with Shell International in London where he was Secretary of the Shell Group Energy Panel and the accredited representative with OPEC, the IEA, the Royaumont Group and the Montreux Energy Forum. In 1991, he was appointed Director-General of the World Petroleum Permanent Council (1991 to 1999). He is currently the Vice-President of the British Institute of Energy Economics, the Director and CEO of the Windsor Energy Group, London and, since 1985, Chairman of the Threadneedle Club.

He is the editor of *International Energy Markets* (1983), *Energy*

Economics in Britain (1983), *The Politics of Middle East Oil* (1993), *An Enduring Friendship* (2006) and *The Arabists of Shemlan – MECAS Memoirs 1944-1978* (2006), and is the author of eight books including *Of the Desert and the Sea*, a personal guide to the Arabian Gulf (1972), *World Petroleum at the Crossroads* (1999) and *Qatar 1967 to 2003 – A Strong New Bridge.* His articles on the global economy, energy, the North Sea and the Middle East have appeared in the *OPEC Bulletin*, the *Bank of England Quarterly Bulletin*, the *Petroleum Review, Energy Policy* and, since 1985, in *Geopolitics of Energy* where he is a member of the Editorial Board.

LORD HOWE OF ABERAVON CH was educated at Winchester College (Exhibitioner) and Trinity Hall, Cambridge (Scholar). He was a Lieutenant in The Royal Signals (1945 to 1948) and after an active contribution to university politics, he was called to the Bar in 1952 and appointed Chairman of the Bow Group in 1955. After twice contesting Aberavon unsuccessfully, he was elected MP for Bebbington in 1964.

He was appointed Solicitor General in 1970 to 1972, Minister for Trade and Consumer Affairs, DTI in 1972 to 1974, Chancellor of the Exchequer in 1979 to 1983, Secretary of State for Foreign and Commonwealth Affairs in 1983 to 1989, Lord President of the Council, Leader of the House of Commons and Deputy Prime Minister from 1989 to 1990.

THE WINDSOR ENERGY GROUP

AIM

The Windsor Energy Group aims to provide a global framework for the public and private sectors to address the strategic issues of energy geo-politics.

STRUCTURE

Membership, by invitation only, is drawn mainly from the major multinational energy companies, and the leading law, finance and security management companies. Meetings are conducted strictly under Chatham House rules. The Group is non profit-making and is financed by annual subscription and sponsorship.

ADVISORY BOARD

The Group programme and reports are steered by an international advisory board of senior diplomats and former diplomats with recognised expertise in global energy matters. The Advisory Board includes high-level diplomats from the United States, Europe, Russia, the Middle East, Latin America, Japan and other areas as considered appropriate. The Board (and Group) is chaired by one or two international figures in the field of the geo-politics of energy.

MEETINGS AND BRIEFING

A three-day meeting is held each year in Windsor Castle and a half-day meeting in the Foreign and Commonwealth Office, London.

Quarterly dinners and briefings for the London diplomatic community are held in London. Other seminars, briefings and reviews are usually requested by an Ambassador or a group of Ambassadors or leading multinational companies for a specific purpose.

MANAGEMENT

Joint Honorary Chairmen:

Lord Howell of Guildford and Sir Graham Boyce

Chief Executive Officer: Paul Tempest

Directors: Ghayth Armanazi; Geoffrey Hancock CMG; Ian Walker and Paul Tempest

WINDSOR ENERGY GROUP ADVISORY PANEL

Ghayth Armanazi *(Arab League Ambassador, London 1992-2000)*, Khaled Al-Duwaisan *(Dean of the London Diplomatic Corps and Ambassador of Kuwait)*, Robert Ebel *(Director of the Center for Strategic International Studies (CSIS, Washington DC)*, Tatsuo Masuda *(ex-Vice-President of Japan National Oil Company, Tokyo)*, Robert Priddle *(ex-Executive Director of the International Energy Agency, Paris)*, Dr Subroto *(ex-Secretary-General of OPEC and ex-Minister of Oil and Energy, Indonesia)*, Arne Walther *(Secretary-General of the World Energy Forum, Riyadh)*, Dr Wang Tao *(ex-President of China National Petroleum Corporation)*.

Administration of the Windsor Energy Group is provided by: MEC International, Granville House, 132 Sloane Street, London SW1X 9AX. Telephone: 020 7591 4816, Fax: 020 7591 4801 Website: www.meconsult.co.uk

SPONSORS

The British Government (Foreign and Commonwealth Office), the Chinese Government, the Japanese Government, NATO, BG (British Gas), BP, Marathon, Mitsui, Petrofac, Petroleos de Venezuela, Shell Petroleum, Rubicon International

ORIGINS OF THE WINDSOR ENERGY GROUP

The Royaumont Group, under the chairmanship of The Hon. Melvin Conant, Washington DC (ex-International Director of the Federal Bureau of Energy, later US Dept. of Energy), held in 1985-93 Annual Consultations under much the same general mandate as the Windsor Energy Group today. The Royaumont Group was supported and attended by Arabian Oil (Tokyo), BP, Compagnie Francaise de Petrole (CFP) Exxon, Mobil, Shell and Texaco. The lead diplomats in the group were: Professor Herman Eilts *(former US Ambassador to Egypt and Saudi Arabia)*, Sir Archie Lamb *(former British Ambassador to Kuwait and Norway)*, Sir John Moberly *(former British Ambassador to Iraq and Jordan)*, Professor Kunio Katakura *(former Japanese Ambassador to UAE, Iraq and Egypt)*.